I0170682

Mourning Coffee for the Mourning Soul

Tracy Renee Lee, GC-C, FD

Copyright © 2014 Tracy Renee Lee

All rights reserved.

ISBN - 0989444732
ISBN - 9780989444736

Tracy Renee Lee

Copyright © 2014 Tracy Renee Lee

All rights reserved.

ISBN - 0989444732
ISBN - 9780989444736

Tracy Renee Lee

DEDICATION

To all souls who mourn.

Tracy Renee Lee

CONTENTS

1	PARENTAL GRIEF	1
2	BLESSINGS	4
3	BROKEN FAMILY	7
4	LIFE AFTER DEATH	9
5	THIS FRIEND	11
6	LOSING YOUR BELOVED	14
7	FOUR PRECIOUS WOMEN	16
8	MOVE ON – A RIDICULOUS TERM	18
9	NEW REALITY	20
10	GRANDMOTHER CONFISCATES CELLPHONES	22
11	SWEET D	25
12	PHASES OF MOURNING	27
13	CAUSE OF DEATH PENDING	29
14	A DAUGHTER'S SACRIFICE	31
15	TRANSFORMATION	33
16	SUICIDE SURVIVORS	35
17	THANKSGIVING	37
18	DEATH COMES IN THREES	39
19	CO-MINGLING	41
20	ROAD TO RECOVERY	43
21	SUICIDE VICTIMS	46

CONTENTS CONTINUED

22 ELEPHANT IN THE ROOM 48

23 STRATEGIES FOR MARITAL BLISS 50

24 MISCARRIAGE 52

25 SUDDEN DEATH 54

26 GRIEF'S PHYSICAL PAIN 57

27 EMBALMING, A SCIENTIFIC PROCESS 59

28 DYING FROM A BROKEN HEART 61

29 WHEN A LOVED ONE HAS BEEN MURDERED 64

30 THE PAIN OF GRIEF 67

31 MISCARRIAGE RECOVERY 69

32 ST. PATTY'S DAY 71

33 HIDDEN TREASURE 73

34 KITTY 76

35 MISSING TODDLER 78

36 CHOOSE RECOVERY 82

37 MAN OF STEEL 85

38 THE OBIT 87

39 THE ARRANGEMENT CONFERENCE 89

40 STILETO JO 92

41 THE UN-DEAD 94

42 GRIEF DESIGNATED AS DISORDER 96

CONTENTS CONTINUED

43	MEMORIAL DAY	99
44	TROPHIES FOR EVERYONE	101
45	I LOVE DAD	103
46	CASKETS I, EXTERIORS	106
47	THE EX-FACTOR	109
48	DECORUM	112
49	PET GRIEF	115
5 0	LOVE ME TENDER	117
51	CASKETS II, CARRYING MECHANISMS	119
52	FUNERAL DIRECTOR FEARS FOR HER LIFE	122
	ABOUT THE AUTHOR	125

ACKNOWLEDGMENTS

I would like to acknowledge my brother for suggesting that I write.
Without his suggestion, I never would have considered it.

Also my husband, who believes I am a great writer.
Without his encouragement,
I would have given up many moons ago.

1

PARENTAL GRIEF

Perhaps the most difficult loss to suffer is that of your child, it stands out as the most dreadful of all. No two people grieve in the exact same manner. This is especially true in the loss of a child. Societal mores dictate a unique set of standards for each of the sexes and this follows true through bereavement. Men are assigned the role of strength while women are allowed to openly express sorrow.

In addition to being a funeral practitioner, I am a portrait artist. In my capacity as an artist, I was working in a large retail store and noticed a young couple checking out at the registers. The husband was attentive to his wife as she paid for their selected items, and assisted her with amazing tenderness and love. She was a stunning beauty and he was strong and handsome. As they walked closer to where I sat, I could see there was something else. I could not remove my gaze from them and to my surprise; they walked right up and sat down at my table. The beautiful woman sat directly across from me. I looked deep into her eyes and was overcome with compassion. It was a very confusing experience. She was perfect in every way, yet there was a vulnerability that tenderly drew you to her. Her gaze was almost yearning and her mind seemed far away. Then her husband spoke. My eyes remained focused on his lovely wife, and then I knew. She sat there, so straight and brave, and without a sound or gasp, a tear streamed down her perfectly formed cheek. As her tear reached her jaw line, I realized that I was looking into the depth of a broken soul. The faraway look that had been so confusing to me was now clear as day. This stunningly beautiful woman had suffered the overwhelming loss of her first-born and only child, just two weeks earlier. Her sweet son had been a vibrant, playful, and beautiful toddler. Their neighbor accidentally ran over him as he retrieved a ball while playing catch with his daddy in the front yard. In an effort to save his son, this strong father sustained dangerous injuries himself and was within 18 inches of reaching his son when the vehicle crushed him beneath its weight. This young mother sat there, not moving, still, and quiet. Her husband recounted the tragic details of their son's death and asked if I could paint his portrait from a cell phone snap that he had taken just days before their loss. I painted their son's portrait. It was beautiful.

This was the first couple I had ever worked with that had suffered the loss of their child, and perhaps that is why it remains with me. I learned so much from these parents. The father was strong, tall, and outgoing; the mother was beautiful, feminine, and withdrawn. Through the years, the daddy has remained strong and outgoing. In fact, as time has passed, I have often worried about his never wavering strength. Conversely, I have witnessed the mother rise and fall as the days have passed. She has displayed her sadness and demonstrated her journey to recovery openly.

For several years now, I have kept in contact with this family. They have since enjoyed the birth of a new child. A girl, as lovely as her mother. Their impact on my funeral practice remains ever strong. They taught me so much about the tragedy of losing a child. They also taught me that two people mourning the same death grieve differently. Each parent had enjoyed unique experiences with their son and each parent grieved in a way that they were able to recover from his tragic death and live as a family again. Their road was so hard, and I am sure it remains so. They are strong and vibrant, yet I observe in quiet moments that they drift back in time and remember how precious and wonderful their son was to them. I learned that society is not necessarily fair, especially to dads when they lose their children. However, most importantly, I learned that if a mom and a dad love and tenderly support each other, each taking care of the other in moments of despair, they will eventually arrive at a place where they can bear the pain. Moreover, although life has forever changed, they can exist together with peace and harmony anew.

2

BLESSINGS

Have you ever known someone and wished you could live in their shoes? Maybe they are famous, maybe they have won the lottery, or maybe they have great luck. Perhaps you know someone whose shoes you would not wish to wear. I know someone like this. She is my cousin.

When we were children, my cousin was scary. She was older than the rest of us and so she was stronger, faster, and smarter than all the little cousins put together. She would pull pranks on us and scare us tremendously. As my cousin grew up, she was a little on the wild side. Probably no wilder than most teenagers, nevertheless she frightened me. As a young woman, my cousin "Got right with God." She became a strong church going woman and married a man from her local area. She had children and her life settled into an average married woman's life. After a while, she divorced her first husband and married a second.

One day at work, I received a notice that my cousin's adult daughter had been in an auto accident. She had been broadsided by an 18-wheeler.

One wonders how she even survived. My cousin immediately gave up her employment and sat day and night at the hospital with her daughter. She prayed incessantly that her daughter would wake from her coma. Nearly a year later, she did. Unfortunately, her daughter must spend her days relearning life's skills. My scary cousin now has custody of her daughter and her daughter's young children. Life will never be the same for any of them.

Soon after her daughter and all of her daughter's life functioning equipment came home, my cousin's father fell ill. Within a very short time, my cousin's father passed away. This was particularly tragic for her because she loved her father so deeply and because her burdens were increased unbelievably. With the death of her father, my cousin assumed the role as leader within her extended family. She now takes care of her disabled daughter, her disabled daughter's very young children, her disabled mother, her ninety-eight year old grandmother, her nieces, and the mistakes and irresponsibility's of her adult siblings. Her burdens are so heavy and so numerous, I don't know how she carries them.

I attended her father's funeral. It was a normal funeral with the usual prayers, music, and sermon from the preacher. During the funeral, my cousin walked up to the pulpit and spoke. To this day, I don't know how she did it. With so many burdens, she spoke of her love for her father and their treasured experiences together. She spoke of the newly acquired responsibilities and burdens that she would now be called upon to bear. She was so vulnerable, so frail and yet so strong all at the same moment. In an instant, she went from scary cousin to superwoman. She pled with her siblings and her husband to help her with these burdens. As she spoke, I thought to myself, my cousin was still the strongest, the fastest, and the smartest of all the cousins put together. My heart was full and I was filled with appreciation and admiration for her.

Nearly three years has passed. This past week at church, my cousin shared her witness of God and her love of Christ. During her witness, she spoke of her dearly departed father, her disabled daughter, her very young grandchildren, her disabled mother, her ninety-eight year old grandmother, her irresponsible siblings, and her nieces.

She called them blessings, not burdens.

3

BROKEN FAMILY

This past week I served a broken family. The father was a strong God-fearing man. He was in his eighties. He was a veteran. He had brought comfort to many during his lifetime.

As many of us do, in his younger years, he had made mistakes. His mistakes lead to a separation in his family. A separation that at his death was insurmountable by his children.

Although this man who had served many during his lifetime has died, the ripple effects of his actions are continuing to affect the living in his absence. Most particularly, his children.

You have always heard, "You hurt the ones you love." Unfortunately, this hurt transcends your death. For those left behind trying to overcome this hurt, your death is not inconsequential. Indeed, pain and suffering are exacerbated by death.

Death does not erase evil deeds against another. If we are the offender, death robs us of the opportunity to make amends and to repair the damages we have inflicted against others; allowing us to rest in peace. If we are the sufferer, death robs us the opportunity to forgive and overcome the damages we have suffered allowing us to live in peace.

It seems likely that this man's family will never recover from his evil deeds against them. How unfortunate that this family of children grew up never experiencing the comfort of their father's strength, never grew up witnessing his good deeds toward others, and never grew up knowing that before all else, he loved them more than life itself. The absence of these experiences creates a void and pathology within the psychological development of the human soul.

The man, who created this family, destroyed this family. His mistakes were probably the same that many of us fall into during our lives. Mistakes that are easy to make yet difficult to repair. This man went to his grave leaving behind him a trail of sadness, heartache, and betrayal. His legacy could have been different. It would have required restitution to his children. It would have required him to take upon himself the consequences of his actions rather than leave his children to suffer them.

As a parent, I want to believe this man tried to repair the destruction he caused within his family. It is impossible for me to comprehend that a parent would go to their grave knowing that they were leaving behind such a mess for their children to live through. The cold hard truth is however, that this is not the first time I have witnessed such devastation within a family caused by one of its own. It is not the first, nor do I believe it will be the last.

Death does not erase evil deeds against another we must do that ourselves.

4

LIFE AFTER DEATH

Recently I had a mother visit me at my funeral home. We had buried her young son just two years earlier. Experiencing the death of your child is a horrific experience. My client, now my friend, had also lost her husband just three months prior to the loss of her son. One can only imagine the pain and anguish through which she has lived.

Her question, "Is there life after death?" surprised me. We had discussed on multiple occasions her belief in an afterlife. As she continued, I realized her question was about her own life. My friend was asking if there would ever come a time when she would experience life as she had before, with joy, love, and security.

Her question is insightful. The experience of loss can become so overwhelming that we forget how to recognize joy and perhaps become fearful of its experience. We may feel uncomfortable in social situations and withdraw from societal encounters. We may feel afraid to experience love again and barricade ourselves from its rapture. These are normal fears and emotions.

Life will never be the same for someone who has lost their child, their life's companion, or anyone of significant value. Such a love loss will never be forgotten nor overcome. Life has changed and eventually you will be able to make adjustments to cope with it.

My friend's experience was tragic, but most likely, she will one day be strong enough to allow love and joy to re-enter her life. She might be a little more guarded, a little more cautious and a little slower to trust, but if she takes care of herself emotionally and spiritually, things will get better. I already see it happening.

Through such an experience, we wonder if there will ever be an end to our sorrow. We may feel there is no hope. My dear friend, there is hope.

So, is there life after death? For the living, indeed there is.

5

THIS FRIEND

I have this friend. She is a unique sort of woman. She is the mother of young children and a computer expert. Actually, I think she might be a computer geek. My association with her began through a women's club membership. It expanded as we attended meetings together, traveled across the great state of Texas for rallies, and generally participated in community improvement activities. I could always tell, there was something underlying about her, but I did not want to get into it. My life was busy enough without meddling into hers. I really just needed her to keep her problems to herself, and she did.

One Saturday afternoon, she called me. Her voice was the same as usual, brightly toned, but void of emotion. She opened our conversation with her usual directness, informing me that her call was in connection to my professional expertise. I offered my standard reply, "Sure, what can I help you with?" I thought she was going to ask me about something she had read on the internet concerning some crazy funeral tradition; but she did not. She shocked me, right there through the phone. Her next statement hit me from left field and I stood there dumb struck. In an instant, I knew I had been a horrible friend. Actually, I had not been a friend at all. I should have listened to the promptings of my heart and reached out to a young woman in a horrible situation, but I did not want to do it. Deep down in my soul, I knew she had problems, but I didn't want to acknowledge them. I did not want to sacrifice my time, nor my efforts, to reach out to someone who was desperately in need of protection and support. To this day, I am ashamed of myself. I put my own concerns, my own time, and the management of my funeral practice, before the needs of someone who truly needed just a little bit of help. I think the slightest effort on my part would have meant the world to her.

As I waited for her question, she bluntly announced that her husband had just shot himself in the brain, and was dead on their apartment floor. I nearly dropped the phone. After a moment of shock, I asked her, "Have you called the Police?" "They are on their way," she replied. "Where are your children?" "In the next room," she said nonchalantly. "Have you called anyone else?" "Pastor is on his way." I could hear the sirens in the background. I told her to let the police and paramedics enter her home. She did. They quickly assessed the situation and whisked her husband off to the hospital. I told her I would meet her there.

Her husband was pronounced DOA. As I entered the emergency room foyer, I could see her walking toward me. She reached out, and latched onto me, as though she were a small child at a horror flick. She gripped me so tightly, breathing frantically, burying her face at the nape of my neck. Everything seemed to slow down to a snail's pace. I brushed away the hair that had fallen into her face. I kissed the crown of her head, and patted her on the back. I coddled her as I would a child, and told her I would help her through this. She was terrified, and the person there to give her comfort, was the woman that had never offered to help her before tragedy struck. She held onto me as though I were her mother. It broke my heart to see her suffer so severely. I was horrified at myself, and I knew that I had been a self-absorbed workaholic; too busy and stressed to assist a friend. How's that for knowing you've messed up in life? She was shaking, yet to those who did not know her, she seemed calm. To me, she was a little girl acting all grown up and brave; but I knew she was terrified. I could see it in her eyes, I could hear it in her voice, and it cut me to the core. She asked me about funeral services, the least expensive possible, and I took him away.

A few days later, we held his service at my funeral home. I was surprised at the number and notable people who attended. This man, who had been horrid to his wife and bothersome in most social situations, had extreme political influence. His unique ability to blog and bend public opinion was very evident by those in attendance.

Thankfully, my friend has found a new life. She seems much happier. She is engaged to be married, has started a computer game business, and has moved to a different state. We keep in touch, mainly through social media. I am thankful her life has found new direction.

In my nightly reflections, my prayers are for the both of us. That her life will be better, that her newly found euphoria will sustain her, and that she will find a better friend to her than I ever was. For me, I pray that I will never allow myself to become so absorbed in my work that I value my time and efforts more than I do the needs of one of God's precious children. Also, that I will be a better friend from this day forward.

Lesson to self: People are in your life for a purpose. Follow the promptings of your heart. No matter how busy you are, take a moment, and offer a helping hand of support. Goodness knows; you may need it yourself someday. Wouldn't it be a pity if the person there to help you, turned out to be just like you? Hum, food for thought.

I am thankful for my friend. She taught me so much about where my life was going. She helped me prioritize life and people, over work and bills. She redirected me back to a better me.

6

LOSING YOUR BELOVED

Many people say that marriage is the hardest part of life. It is not. Surviving the death of your beloved requires more work, deeper suffering, and greater endurance than marital bliss ever asked from anyone.

Surviving your beloved is excruciating and arduous. Experts in the study of grief have expressed theory upon theory to aid survivors through this journey. The fact remains however, that theory is not fact. In searching for a yellow brick road to recovery, you must realize, as did Dorothy and her cohorts, that you already possess the strength and ability to survive. Identify your strengths and cultivate them. Utilize your abilities and realize that you are the only one capable of surmounting your grief. From this point forward, it is your job to continue onward without the companionship of your beloved. You must redefine your role in a myriad of life's situations as your own provider, your own protector, and your own strategist. If your loss is recent, it will take some time before you are able to embark on your proactive road to recovery.

Centuries ago, society required survivors to wear black for one year after the death of their loved ones. From this tradition, we wonder, does it take only one year to recover from the loss of a lifetime of love? Grief is the price we pay for the gift of love. I wish I could tell you that one year of grief is all that you will suffer. I cannot.

If you loved your spouse with the depth of your soul, grief may forever be your unwelcome companion.

7

FOUR PRECIOUS WOMEN

Four precious women came to my office. Although they were sorrowful, they filled my funeral home with joy. This was the day they had known would come; they were prepared both mentally and spiritually. Between the four of them, the loss was great. They had not only lost their father, husband, and grandpa; they had lost their spiritual leader. The man in my parlor, while living, had been a Reverend. His congregation had been small in number, but large in kindness, generosity, and acceptance. As we worked through the details of laying the Reverend to rest, this darling family of women, cooperated and supported each other with softness and love. These four precious women were a true testament to his work.

Through the days that followed, the girls served their mother, and each other, with tenderness. Their parishioners, one by one, came to the funeral home, and one by one, did so with kindness, respect, and compassion. Indeed, the Reverend's influence seems to have emulated the light of Christ to those he served.

During the week of this man's death, these four precious women, demonstrated flawless virtue and goodness. My heart grew with respect, admiration, and love for them. My conviction in Christ's mission was magnified, and my hope for humanity was shored up.

The Reverend's final resting place was not where he had lived, and so necessity dictated that he travel a great distance for interment. I was hesitant to see these four precious women embark upon the final leg of their journey, but knew they had an errand of love to fulfill. Therefore, as I bid them farewell, my prayers and love went with them.

These four precious women, who came to my office, suffering the greatest pain that we as humans endure, left it filled with joy. I am grateful to them for sharing their time with me, for exemplifying the light of Christ, and for baring their wounds with grace and dignity. Although this week was caused by a solemn occasion, my soul was lifted, my joy was increased, and my cup was filled.

Even in his death, the Good Reverend's work lives on.

8

MOVE ON, A RIDICULOUS TERM

There comes a time after you have lost a loved one that others want you to move on. Some think it is unhealthy for you to continue grieving over someone who is gone. Although misguided, at least these people have your best interest at heart. Others are just uncomfortable with death and want you to get over it as you would a cold or the flu. They want you to put it away in a neat little box so that they do not have to be inconvenienced or uncomfortable whenever they see you. This subject begs the question "Is there a time to move on."

It is important to realize that you are the authority on the subject of your recovery timeline. No one can, nor should tell you how and when to feel better, when to get over it, or when to move on. No one except you had your experiences with the deceased. No one can possibly understand the depth of your experiences with the deceased. No one knows your ability to overcome the loneliness and sometimes fear associated with your loss. At times, you may even feel anger. Anger at the deceased for leaving you alone, anger at yourself for something you did or did not do before they were gone, anger at others for something they did or did not do. Feelings of anger are natural and are quite often followed by feelings of guilt. Guilt can be destructive because it can damage self-esteem. On the other hand, it can be motivating in that it may encourage you not to repeat such actions ever again. Most often though, guilt feelings are actually feelings of regret. If you realize that your guilt is actually regret, your self-esteem may recover more easily.

If you have a friend or loved one pushing you to move on, analyze their motives. If their motives are purely in your best interest, take an objective look at your situation. Has your grief become debilitating for an extended amount of time? If so, it may be time to seek out a source for counseling. Debilitating grief is called complicated grief. Once things have become complicated, it might be advantageous to have someone help you regain order in your life. Remember, the death of a loved one requires a completely new structure in your functionality. It may take quite some time for you to adjust to your new requirements in life. Statistically, it takes on average, 3 years for a widow to recover to a comparable level of functionality after the death of her husband. Unfortunately, for a widower, the outlook is a little bleaker.

The most important things to remember are that you will never forget your loved one, you will never stop loving your loved one, and you will never replace your loved one. There will most likely come a time when you will be able to overcome the devastation of your loss. A time when you will be able to function in your daily activities without crying or withdrawing. Nevertheless, when you love someone, they are forever a part of your existence.

In other words, we never move on, we simply live on.

9

NEW REALITY

Often times, when you experience the loss of a significant loved one, you feel as though you are dreaming, and that you might suddenly wake up to find that all is well. This past week, I have had two clients tell me that the passing of their loved one did not feel real to them. They were both surprised when I told them, that what they were experiencing was normal.

When you experience such a devastating loss, your body will react in such a way, that you may feel as though you are dreaming. Perhaps you feel as though the life you are living is not your own. This reaction is a safety mechanism that protects your psychological and physical well-being. If our bodies did not do this for us, the pain of such a significant loss would be too much to bear, and we might possibly perish ourselves. The numbing of our senses, allows us to get through the immediate pain of our loss, without a complete void in our functionality. It is incumbent on us to make important decisions at this time, and we would not be able to do so, if the pain were not somehow masked. The realization of your loss will manifest itself soon enough, and your loss and loneliness may significantly hamper your functionality for quite some time. Realizing that all of this is very normal, may help you to accept the loss, and focus on recovery.

Recovery from a loved one's loss is difficult, and may be lengthy. Take the time to appreciate your loved one, and the joy and enrichment they brought into your life while they were living. Grief can be difficult to overcome, and it never completely goes away. Grief is the price we pay for love. You will never stop loving your loved one, so you will never stop grieving. With time however, life will get easier and return to some level of normality.

It is important to remember, that you still have others in your life, who need and deserve your love. Love brings joy back into our lives. Embrace the love you have for those around you, and allow them to help you overcome the pain you are experiencing.

Although you will continue to grieve your loss, loving others will help your recovery.

10

GRANDMOTHER CONFISCATES CELLPHONES

Today I visited with a dear woman that I met about 3 months ago. My visits with her on both occasions were to discuss her funeral arrangements. My first visit with her took place in her hospital room. It was a very uncomfortable day for her and I left the hospital praying that her doctors would be able to discover the cause of her ailments and offer her some relief. She was a sweet woman and even though she was in severe pain, she was friendly and concerned with my comfort.

Today, as I visited her at her home, she was much more comfortable than before. Her landscape was cheerful and expressed her personality through brightly colored blossoms. There was a peaceful arbor spreading shade over a sweet table with seating for two. Other flowering bushes offered privacy and shared their pleasing fragrance with anyone willing to take a moment to enjoy the pleasant bounty of spring.

Before discussing the business of the day, we spoke of her past few months. She told me about her illness and her plans for her future. We discussed her recent activities with her children and grandchildren.

Recently she held a slumber night with her 15 grandchildren. She chose a small space and confiscated each child's electronic devices, to ensure interaction and intimacy. Board games and waffles were abundant; TV's, cell phones and I-pads were non-existent. Each of her grandchildren began the evening with complaints of impending boredom. Each of her grandchildren closed the event with a new appreciation of love and precious memories created with their grandmother.

I know that this activity was difficult and painful for her to host. Her health is fragile and she suffers extreme pain. She understands what is coming though, and she is systematically preparing her loved ones for her passing. She is actively creating memories for each of them, so that once she dies; they will have a treasured moment with her to call their own.

In my own life, I often reflect back to experiences with my grandmother. She also took time to create moments that taught her descendants strength and brought them peace. As a grandmother myself, I compare my actions against those of my grandmother. I try to live up to her generosity, her kindness, and her love for her grandchildren. I try to create memories with my grandchildren that will one day help them surmount the difficulties, trials and weaknesses that plague the human race.

This woman's family is blessed with her wisdom and her courage to create peace, love, and confidence for them in her last few months of life. She is a strong and brilliant woman.

I often see families where loved ones do not have such thoughtful memories to draw upon. The lack of sweet familial experiences creates contention and self-doubt among descendants. Regardless of where you are in life, take the opportunity to create sweet memories with those you love. This dear woman is fortunate enough to know that her life will soon end, and dedicated enough to sacrifice her comfort for the future of those she loves. Sadly, this is not always the case near the end of life. Without notice, the grim reaper can call your number, and within a twinkling of an eye, life is over. Enjoy every moment you have with your family. Never waste an opportunity to express your love for them. If you do so, your family and loved ones will be better prepared for life without you by their side. They will face life with greater confidence and in times of weakness, they will be able to deflect temptation and heartache. They will survive, secure in their knowledge that you loved and provided for them, all that you could.

11

SWEET D

I visited with a woman today who suffers a terminal illness. The ravages of her illness are painful and will soon take her life from her. This weighs heavy on her mind, not for herself, but for those she loves. Sweet D has completely accepted her impending demise, but worries immensely about its effect on her children and grandchildren. She tries to talk to them about what is going to happen, but they refuse to hear it. She asked me if I would help them through it, once she dies. I answered, "Of course I would." Her heart is broken. She wants to prepare her family for her death. She does not understand why they will not face the reality of her future.

Human nature is a crazy thing. Each of us has different strengths and weaknesses. As I spoke with Sweet D, I told her that her children and grandchildren love her deeply. In fact, the depth of their love is what causes them to deny the reality that she is dying. Denial creates a barrier of protection against the severe pain inflicted through loss and death. Her family will wait until she dies to consider that there will be a time when she no longer lives next door.

Sadly, Sweet D feels alone, abandoned and unloved. The denial of her family to accept her impending death creates a barrier between them. She is left alone to contemplate what she might experience after her life passes. She is left alone to plan her funeral. She is left alone in moments of fear, trial, and weakness. She is left alone to mourn the loss of her life, and any future experiences with her children and grandchildren. Sweet D's family has not yet realized that they are not just losing her; she is losing them. Her loss is infinitely more devastating than their loss. They are losing one family member. She is losing every family member.

If someone you love has received a short-term diagnosis, denial may be your close friend. This is a natural reaction to devastating news. It is important however, to realize that the person dying may need you to help them through the experience and fear of knowing that death is at their doorstep. Their knowledge that they will soon die, affects them severely. They may be happy and then sad, they may be fearful and then fearless. Their emotions and fears may be all over the rector scale. The advance knowledge of death's closeness may bring about personality and philosophical changes. If possible, put your fear and denial aside. Reach out to your loved one and be there for them. Open your heart and comfort them through the experience of dying. Although the experience may be excruciatingly painful for you, once they pass, you alone will have comfort through the precious moments you spent together. Most likely, you will find the experience to be life changing and spiritually enlightening. Many of us fear the experience of death. How sweet it would be for the dying, in their last months of life, to have the strength and love of a loved one to draw upon.

Dying alone is tragic, especially when those you love stand beside you.

12

PHASES OF MOURNING

I often hear people refer to a teenager's poor behavior as a phase. Somehow, this interpretation or usage of the word lessens its true application. A phase as described in the dictionary is a process of change or development. This true meaning of "phase" is exactly what we are describing in the Phases of Mourning. Each phase as it is accomplished brings the survivor back to a balance in life. It allows joy, peace, and tranquility to return. It reestablishes harmony and allows functionality to exist within the survivor's life.

Mourning is divided into four phases.

Phase 1 - A PERIOD OF NUMBNESS. Numbness is the deprivation of physical or emotional sensations. The numbness experienced by most survivors, helps them to disregard that death has occurred. This short period of numbness allows them to function in a manner close to their normal level of productivity. This is particularly noteworthy, as there are very important decisions to make at this time.

Phase 2 - A PERIOD OF YEARNING. The survivor yearns for the return of the deceased and does not yet comprehend the permanence of this new reality. Anger is generally experienced during this phase. Anger may be directed at the deceased for not being there to help out, or for inflicting loneliness and pain upon the survivor. Anger may also be directed at others for not doing something to prevent the death of the deceased. It may also be projected upon others or self, for non-factually based perceptions, affecting the cause of death. Anger is a powerful and motivating emotion. It is not always factually based.

Phase 3 - A TIME OF DISORGANIZATION AND DISPAIR. The survivor is learning that things are not the same. They find it difficult to function as they once did. Each experience that was once a cooperative effort is now their sole responsibility. This is the most crucial phase of the experience to overcome. If a survivor is unable to move beyond this phase, they are in danger of entering severe depression and recovery may become extremely complicated.

Phase 4 - A REORGANIZATION OF BEHAVIOR. In this phase of mourning, we see the survivor change all aspects of their existence. They pull their lives together and begin to function at their normal capacity, albeit alone.

Although life has forever changed, if a survivor passes through each of these phases successfully, grief recovery will be clinically completed. They should be able to satisfactorily accomplish their daily activities and eventually participate in social activities with greater ease.

13

CAUSE OF DEATH PENDING

At times, a death certificate may be issued with the cause of death listed as pending. This generally happens when an investigation is taking place and the cause of death is in question. Death certificates are necessary for legal, financial and real estate purposes. Most applications do not require cause of death, the exception to this rule is of course insurance. If your insurance policy has an accidental death rider, you will want to file for an amended death certificate after cause of death has been determined.

Filing for an amended death certificate is easily accomplished. In most cases, you need only contact your local registrar, fill out the necessary forms, pay the required fees, and amended death certificates will be issued.

The difficulties associated with "cause of death pending" are the unresolved questions of the family. Parents, children, and spouses find it difficult to understand and recover when the cause of death is pending. Acceptance is the last stage of Dr. Kubler-Ross' five stages of grief. For most people, the death of a loved one is the ultimate trauma experienced in life. If the cause of death is pending, the family may find it difficult to begin the work of acceptance. If acceptance is unobtainable, complicated grief may become a reality. Complicated grief is the prolonged suffering of a survivor. Complicated grief may affect the functionality of the survivor.

Generally, the cause of death will be revised once the investigation has been completed. There are however certain circumstances where cause of death may not be determinable. In such a case, family and close friends may find it very difficult to recover. If you are suffering this type of loss, you may find it helpful to join a support group or to seek out a counselor. Your funeral director should be able to help you find various organizations that focus on helping the bereaved through such extreme circumstances. Your road to recovery may be slow and arduous. You may think there is no hope. You may find yourself filled with despair. My dear friend, do not allow yourself to continue on without intervention. There are people and organizations willing and waiting to help you. Do not do this alone. It is too difficult. Allow those around you who love and care for you, to lend a helping hand. If you do so, you will realize that there is hope and love abounding. Family and friends love and care for you. Allow them the opportunity to help.

14

A DAUGHTER'S SACRIFICE

This story is about a brave soul who is fearless and committed to service. She is a courageous woman of strength, loyalty, and sacrifice. She lives in a very small town where everyone knows everyone, and everyone knows your business.

She is a daughter in a rather large family. Both of her parents are in the same nursing home together. They share a great love for each other and their daughter respects that. She gets up every morning and goes to the nursing home to care for her parents. She washes them, she feeds them, she takes them for outings, and most of all, she loves them. At the end of the day, when all is quiet, my friend carries home her parent's laundry. She painstakingly washes their laundry, and returns to the nursing home the next day, with fresh linens and undies for her dear mom and dad. From the depth of her soul, she is committed to her parents. To their dying day, she sacrifices and cares for their every need. The interesting part of this story though, is yet to be told. My dear friend lives in a town where her siblings also live.

On any given day, I can drop by the nursing home, and there will be my dear friend, caring for her sweet parents. Sadly, she has always been alone in her commitment. One wonders why one child over the others is committed beyond reproach.

Her father passed last year and my dear friend took care of every detail for his service. She made arrangements for her dear mother to attend, and she ensured the comfort of all friends and family attending. I do not think until that time, I had realized the depth of her commitment, her love and her sacrifice on behalf of her darling parents.

I read a message today on social media. Paraphrasing it said, "Recovery from the loss of a loved one is like learning how to dance with a limp." This is so true. Recovery from the loss of someone we love so dearly, is similar to the recovery of a broken leg. Although the bone mends itself, it is never as it was before. If may function well enough to walk briskly, but dancing exposes the injury.

My girlfriend's siblings dance through life without a thought or sacrifice for the parents. Nevertheless, my girlfriend sacrifices her days, and even her nights, for her parents. She never dances. She has neither the time nor the energy to dance. She shields her parents from the limp in her heart, which is the realization of their mortality. Even in the final hours of her father's life, she shielded him from the fear and sadness that weighs so heavily upon her soul.

Her mother lives on. My friend is by her side day in and day out. She will continue to be there, until the day, her mother's soul leaves this earth, and joins her husband, in the presence of their beloved maker. I am sure they will enjoy a reunion of great joy and love. I think they might even enjoy a dance together. I wonder, might my friend share a dance with her husband, that same day? A dance to honor her sacrifice and to rejoice at the return of her freedom.

My friend is a devoted daughter. When the day comes that she can dance, I know it will be with a severe, yet well-earned limp.

15

TRANSFORMATION

The loss of a parent can be very devastating. At such a time, we realize so many things. We understand that we no longer have our parent to call for help or advice. At the same time, we realize that we are now the eldest person in our lineage. We are now the person that others rely on for advice, experience, acceptance, and love. We have suddenly become the custodian of our legacy. We accept the responsibilities of keeping our family together, keeping them safe, and moving them toward a better life. The torch of responsibility passes from one generation to the next as the breath of life and soul exists our parent's body. Earlier today, I witnessed the passing of the torch in my cousin's family.

Today was her mother's funeral. My cousin, ever strong, spoke at her mother's funeral as she did at her father's just three years earlier. As my cousin spoke of the love and lessons her mother had taught her, I could hear her breath quiver. I marveled at her strength. I remembered our earlier years as children when we would play at my great grandmother's home. My cousin would lead our small band of cousins as we struggled to play in harmony together. As I sat in the congregation, my eyes scanned those attending. I noticed that most of us, our little play group of cousins, were in attendance. As my cousin spoke, I could see each of our play group empathize with her excruciating experience.

My cousin is so strong. She has been tempered at her Makers hand. She has suffered extreme trials and burdens and she has learned great lessons. They have made her the amazing woman that she is today. I have no doubt that my cousin will exercise great leadership with her family. They are fortunate to have her wisdom, her strength, and her unconditional love to draw upon in times of weakness, self-doubt, or need.

My cousin loved her mother. She respected and appreciated her mother. As she spoke, I witnessed a unique and marvelous transformation. Today, my cousin accepted the passing of her mother's torch and became the custodian for her family group. She now carries the responsibility for her lineage's heritage. She will do a fine job, of that I am sure. Through the trials of her life, she has suffered extreme difficulties and extreme joys. Her experiences have well prepared her for this new phase of life. She will have moments of weakness, self-doubt, anger, and despair. They will be out weighted by the joy that comes from service and sacrifice for others.

16

SUICIDE SURVIVORS

Suicide is a very complex tragedy for family and friends of the deceased. When a loved one intentionally kills him or herself, confusion and intense guilt are immediately present among the survivors. Interestingly enough, in cases of suicide, mere acquaintances may also identify with these feelings. Survivors will second-guess themselves, questioning why they did not see the signs. They will ponder and try to recall little nuances. They will blame themselves, for not identifying, and acting upon what now seems as obvious attempts from the deceased, to reach out for help.

Survivors will try to discover a reason for the suicide. Sometimes the reasons are obvious. The deceased may have alluded to their intentions, they may have displayed classic signs of pre-suicidal behaviors, or they may have suffered something tragic that pushed them beyond their coping abilities. In such circumstances, survivors may have tried to intervene without success. Failure to stave off the suicide may cause feelings of inadequacy.

Sometimes the reasons for suicide are not obvious. If survivors did not recognize suicidal signs, or try to intervene, the suicide may bring on overwhelming guilt, fear, or self-loathing. This is a dangerous time for survivors. Often, they are suffering similar issues, and additional suicides are a great risk. In search of answers, survivors will begin to speculate; they will begin to play the blame game. Whether blame is internalized, or directed against others, it can be deadly.

Identifying the clinical reasons for suicide can be very helpful. It offers survivors an identifiable cause for the tragedy. If pathological illness is identified, others may be more readily accepting of intervention. The goal in identifying the reasons for suicide, is to diminish intense unwarranted guilt, extreme hopelessness, and most importantly, prevent additional suicides among the survivors.

17

THANKSGIVING

I had a dear friend die this past year. Although he passed away in a different state, I go to his social media page and leave him messages every now and then. I miss him so terribly, because he was an amazing human being. His heart was true and good, and he was honest with his fellow man and with himself. He was a friend to my family, and when you met him, you loved him, because of his goodness. My friend died smack dab in the middle of Thanksgiving and Christmas. How like him, he died in the season of family tradition and giving, two things he revered.

It would be easy to be miserable this year, thinking of how much we miss our dear friend, but he would not want that. Instead, we will remember all of the good that he contributed during his short life. We will be thankful for the time we had with him, the growth he inspired in us, his kindness, his generosity and for his passion for truth.

I read his obituary today, for the first time. It spoke volumes about my friend. It mentioned his accomplishments, which were many; and then, there was a paragraph that told who he was. *"Preston always stood up for correct principals. He was a scriptorian, loved music, upheld the Constitution, big on self-sufficiency and was courageous and undaunted." (Richfield Reaper, December 2012)* I am thankful for so many things, and although I may shed a tear that he is gone, I will forever remain grateful for the influence of my dear friend, and the example he set for me.

The holidays can be a very difficult time for someone who has lost a loved one, especially if this is his or her first holiday season since the loss. Even though we try to focus on how much better our lives are for having had our loved one, we miss them so terribly, that it is difficult to experience the cheer of the season.

If you know someone suffering through his or her first holiday season after loss, please be mindful of him or her. This is a particularly difficult time and they may feel lonely and isolated. Take a moment to remember with them, the wonderful moments of life they shared with their loved one. Participate in family traditions and create new ones that honor their deceased. Your blessings will be great, and you will have helped someone through a time, when your good acts of kindness were priceless.

That is what my friend Preston would have done.

18

DEATH COMES IN 3'S

As a girl, I remember hearing my mother and grandmother always saying, "Death comes in threes." I found this to be a terrifying statement. As a funeral director, I now understand how this old saying, coincides with the risk of death multiplicity within families and friendship groups.

Bereavement is a state of sorrow over the death of a loved one. When we are bereaved, we suffer a host of ailments ranging from appetite disturbances and sadness, to migraines and depression. Bereavement can become complicated and extended for many survivors. Generally, survivors will feel desolate or alone for a period of time. Navigating back to a healthy state of living is essential for the survivor. If this is not accomplished, difficulties, illnesses and even death may follow.

It is an interesting phenomenon that one person's death can cause another person's death. As a funeral director, I have witnessed this phenomenon firsthand. I have seen spouses die within hours of each other, siblings pass at the funerals of their brothers or sisters and sweethearts commit suicide after learning their beloved has done so.

These deaths caused by other deaths are not the norm; however, they happen. The elderly and the infirmed tend to be at risk due to the incredible levels of stress and sorrow induced by loss. The mentally ill or those with mental retardation may find themselves at an even greater risk. One's risk is relative to their level of dependency and attachment on the deceased. Their physical and mental health may also contribute to their risk factor. If one is aware that they, or someone they know, fall into these categories, seeking support and medical intervention early on, might be wise.

There are also moments in time, which place the survivor at increased risk. The moment of death notification, if unexpected, can be very stressful. If you are notifying a family or friend of a loved one's death, evaluate the significance of their attachment and any possible health risks. If someone has a heart condition, or some other significant health issue, you might take precautionary measures as recommended by their physician before proceeding.

The initial trip to the funeral home can also be a very stressful moment. Not only might the survivor be highly stressed over the financial weight of the funeral, they may not be prepared to speak so bluntly about their loss. They may be poorly prepared for the arrangement conference and feel uneasy making legal decisions at such a vulnerable time. Unfortunately, each consecutive trip to the funeral home generally increases the level of stress on the survivor. Funeral week is filled with emotional turmoil, insecurities, financial hardship and even familial bickering. All of these issues increase stress on one's physical and mental wellness.

Does death come in threes? It's possible, but now we know how to evaluate risk factors. With this knowledge, the statements made by my mother and grandmother, are not nearly so frightening. As an adult, I can evaluate attachment levels and health discrepancies. I am able to deliver such tragic news to my family members with greater understanding of risk factors, and can incorporate relevant efforts to preserve the lives of those I love so dearly.

19

CO-MINGLING

Ground burial has long been the traditional choice for interment in America. In recent years however, cremation has become a viable choice, among the adventurous baby boomers. As they prepare for their final expenses, many questions arise. One question, in particular, is asked more often than any other, "Can my pet be cremated with me?"

It is illegal to co-mingle human cremains. In other words, two humans, may not be cremated in the same chamber, at the same time. Likewise, it is illegal, to cremate an animal, where human beings are cremated. Plainly speaking, your pet may not be cremated, at the same crematorium, where you may be cremated.

As a licensed funeral director, I often witness family members slipping mementos into a loved one's casket, immediately before it is closed. In fact, I recently observed a very young nephew, slip a little wooden box, into his Uncle's casket. The box had a doggy paw engraved upon it, next to the name, "Love." It was a very touching moment, and caused me to think seriously about my own pet's living situation, when my time comes to meet my maker.

As with interment, inurnment (the process of placing cremains in an urn), offers unique choices, to achieve your final wishes. One might choose an appropriate location where their cremains, and the cremains of their pet, might be sprinkled together. An appropriate choice might be the old oak tree at his or her family home place. If one has chosen to have their cremains buried, a double cremation vault might be an appropriate selection. A double cremation vault encases two urns of cremains. One urn might encase the master's cremains, the other urn might encase the pet's cremains.

If you find yourself in this unique situation, you will need to have the assistance of a very special someone to accomplish your final wishes. It may just turn out, that your very young nephew, surprisingly steps forward to accomplish this final act of "Love" for you and your pet. My best advice: "Be kind to animals, and to your very young nephews. Sometimes even the tiniest humans turn out to be our biggest champions."

20

ROAD TO RECOVERY

When a family experiences a death, almost every member of the household mourns, including the family dog. There are positive and proven ways that help one cope and recover from the loneliness and depression experienced with the death of a loved one. It is important to keep in mind however, that not everyone mourns nor recovers in the exact same way.

Exercise is good for the heart, body and soul. A 20 to 40 minute aerobic activity results in improvement in the survivor's state of mind. A vigorous pumping heart decreases anxiety, lifts the mood and creates a positive experience that persists for several hours. Psychological benefits associated with exercise are a welcome bonus for the bereaved. They are comparable to the gains found with standard forms of psychotherapy.

Religion offers hope for the future and forgiveness for the past. It also offers likeminded support and understanding. It can be a source for counseling and re-socialization, a gateway back to recovery.

Family and friends can be a great resource for recovery. Traveling to visit loved ones in other areas or having them visit the survivor, offers companionship that is familiar, uplifting and relative to their life's experiences.

Hobbies occupy the mind and hands. They engage our brains and keep them in good health. Hobbies create a sense of accomplishment. They propel us toward a healthier and happier recovery.

Psychotherapy is sometimes warranted. Counseling can help a survivor identify habits and encourage positive growth. It can yield a recovery plan that the survivor is unable to identify, implement and accomplish on his or her own.

A support group is a scheduled gathering of people with common experiences and concerns. It provides emotional and moral support, as well as new perspectives on life, increased understanding of grief, and close personal ties.

Traditions are also a wonderful tool for grief recovery. Observing traditions that were once enjoyed with the deceased, helps up accept that they are gone from us physically, yet with us still, through the activities and love we shared together. Such activities, now traditions, will aid your family by anchoring them securely to their heritage. Observing traditions stabilizes a family through loss, expansion and changing environments.

Animal companionship typically results in fewer migraines and less persistent fears. Fewer phobias, lower levels of panic, and less drug and alcohol intake are very positive side effects associated with our furry friends. The love and acceptance of a pet, helps us to combat depression and isolation. If you have a family pet, be mindful of their needs. Taking Fido out for a brisk walk will provide both of you healthier opportunities for exercise, socialization and companionship.

People have a strong need for communication and companionship. Through support groups, church, friends and family we are able to recall, reclaim and rekindle our most cherished memories. Moreover, through these relationships and activities, we are able to begin our recovery.

As Christmas is upon us, it is even more important that we offer our companionship to those we know who have lost a loved one this past year. Important dates are the most difficult to endure when we are bereaved. If you can find it within your heart, I would encourage you to take a moment to visit or call someone you know who is facing the holidays without the companionship of their loved one. Reflect for a moment the sadness you would feel in their situation. Be thankful for your cheer and share a moment of life with someone who has suffered the sorrows of death.

21

SUICIDE VICTIMS

Suicide is tragic and it spikes around the holidays each year. As a funeral director, I see families suffering suicide loss year after year. Not only are they suffering the loss of their loved one, they are suffering an internal strife of blame and guilt.

The holiday season is a time full of tradition and family heritage. Depressed individuals generally complain of feeling empty inside and alone. With the rich focus on belonging and love at this time of year, those suffering depression may not be able to endure the activities, traditions and heritage surrounding them. The juxtaposition of their feelings or perceptions, to the merry holiday festivities, may indeed lead them to end their life. To endure such an extreme loss at this time of year is particularly harrowing.

Nearly 750,000 individuals commit suicide yearly (Worden, 2009). Statistics show that those who have suffered a suicidal loss may be at risk of suicide themselves. If you have thoughts of suicide, or if you are contemplating such an action, immediately seek intervention. Do not hint or allude to your intentions or difficulties. Be specific and immediately reach out to a medical or suicide intervention facility. Dial 911, tell them you need help, get yourself to the emergency room, and allow someone to intervene for you. Remember, although you might not love yourself, you are loved by others. Even though you cannot recognize it now, you have value, and there will be those who will sorely mourn your loss.

Depression can be a deadly condition, but it is also preventable. The goal in crime-prevention is to separate the criminal from the victim, before a heinous crime is committed. In suicide, the victim and the perpetrator are the same person. Physically, it is impossible to separate them. Psychological and medical interventions are very effective anti-crime tools for thwarting suicide. If an alert individual is able to identify a suicidal person, or if a suicidal person will identify him or herself and seek help, a life may be saved, a crime may be prevented, and a family may remain whole.

22

ELEPHANT IN THE ROOM

I am an experienced funeral practitioner, and to this day, even though I do not mean to, and I really should not, I still hesitate, when I see a friend or family member, who has recently lost a loved one. With all of the people I serve on a daily basis, one would think, I would have moved beyond that momentary awkwardness, when coming face to face, with a grieving friend.

Why do we experience awkwardness, avoid or even ignore our grieving friends? Is it because we fear inflicting further pain? Perhaps we fear our inability to console. Is it that we feel tongue-tied? Could it be we just do not know what to say? Maybe we fear making our friend cry. Whatever the reasons, we need to understand, that our awkward reactions, do not help our grieving friends. Indeed, these reactions have the opposite effect on them. Our failure to recognize and respond to our grief stricken friends actually inflicts additional pain on them. Alas, try as I might, overcoming this brief moment of hesitation, remains difficult for me, almost impossible actually, and I imagine it does for you too.

I have learned over the years that the most important thing I can do for a friend who mourns the loss of their loved one, is simply act normally. Understanding that this is impossible, I have moved beyond my weakness to do so, and have chanced upon the best alternative. "Acknowledge the elephant in the room."

Mourners want and need most of all, to talk about their loss. They need to work through what has happened to them. Talking with someone who knows them and will not judge them, allows them to accept that death has happened, to realize that there is a new reality in which they must function, and redirects them to work out their road to recovery.

Do not be alarmed. This does not mean that every grieving acquaintance you have, will want to carry on a detailed conversation with you, about his or her loss. A simple acknowledgement is more than sufficient. "I was sorry to hear about your dad," offers an acquaintance comfort. Those same words, spoken to a dear friend, offer an appropriate opportunity for a healing conversation.

As the year closes, and we look forward to the new one, I would suggest that you add this resolution to your list.

"Recognize the elephant in the room."

If you will, you and your grief stricken friends will benefit from its practice. You will also find that your discomfort is greatly lessened around the bereaved.

23

STRATEGIES FOR MARITAL BLISS

Prior to our marriage, my husband had been married once before. After his first marriage failed, he developed a strategy for marital bliss that he faithfully applies to our marriage. The first rule in his "Strategies for Marital Bliss" is, "Never go to bed angry, upset or annoyed at your spouse." Seems simple enough, unless, of course, one has ever been married. Through the years, however, anger, discontent and annoyance have never been a significant problem for us. The reason, I imagine, is directly related to his second strategy for marital bliss.

During the 1960's, the "flower children" coined a phrase, "Love is never having to say you're sorry." My husband's second strategy for marital bliss is in direct conflict with this philosophy. His second strategy is "Regardless of fault; love rushes to say sorry, first."

My husband's "Strategies for Marital Bliss" actually apply to every relationship between human beings. Whether you are sweethearts, siblings, relatives, co-workers or acquaintances, you should seriously consider incorporating his rules, into every relationship in which you participate. While it is true that none of us is perfect, at the moment of death, imperfection is frozen. Death robs the living of the opportunity for simple resolution and blocks the comfort of peace.

These lost opportunities for resolution and peace are unfortunate indeed. This undesirable state of affairs creates years of complicated grief for the bereaved survivor. The depth of stress brought on by this situation can lead to serious ailments. My best advice is to follow my husband's "Strategies for Marital Bliss" in one's everyday interactions and in every relationship in which one engages.

If one finds that he or she is at odds with a loved one, or with anyone for that matter, try to incorporate my husband's strategies into the relationship. Even in the worst of circumstances, clearing one's own slate of any blame, will in the end, clear one's conscious. I am certainly not advocating that a victim apologize to a perpetrator for any abuse or crime inflicted upon them. What I am suggesting, is that you try to forgive. Forgiveness will bring you the most comfort possible. Do not continue the cycle of victimization at your own hands. Do what is best for you, by releasing the negative stresses of anger and hate.

Once a death has occurred, victims become the unexpected losers, giving the obnoxious or abusive acquaintance, indefinite power over them. Due to their own inability to resolve their lives, the victim has perpetuated the negative control that will hamper their recovery until they are able to effect resolution within themselves. This is an extremely difficult feat to accomplish. Turn your woes into a winning scenario; deal with the abuse while your abuser remains living. Clear your life of them and their negative control over your happiness.

In the case of a failed marriage, no matter who is at fault, both parties lose. The same is true in life and death. Do not rob yourself of peace, do not rob yourself of happiness and certainly, do not rob yourself of bliss. Follow my husband's strategies; take care of unfinished business today before your head hits the pillow. Your life will be better for it.

24

MISCARRIAGE

A miscarriage is the death of a baby in the womb. It is tragic for the couple losing their child, for the immediate family and their closely extended family. Outside of this small family circle, however, the loss is barely recognized. Unfortunately, society fails to recognize this loss of life as a death of any significance. The life of the unborn is whittled down in value as a non-loss. Other losses falling into this category of non-loss are socially unspeakable losses. Examples would be suicidal loss, death caused by embarrassing activities, or deaths of secret liaisons. Under these circumstances, the grief experience is disenfranchised because the death situation is neither socially sanctioned nor significant.

If a mother loses her baby prior to birth, others will not experience the reality of the child's existence. Her grief and that of her husband will not be acknowledged beyond the close inner circles of their family. In this situation, the mother and father are expected to carry on with life as though nothing grievous has happened. Reality, however is very different for the parents of the lost pregnancy. They have experienced the woes and joys of pregnancy, the anticipation of the expansion of their family, and most likely have made changes to their home in anticipation of the sweet arrival. Their life has changed with the expectation of their child being born. The spontaneous or induced loss of a child creates a void that fills with heartache and grief.

Re-enfranchisement of grief is critical for the parents. Helpful intervention would include assisting the couple in talking about, and exploring their thoughts and feelings over their loss. They must be able to express and experience the fact that death has occurred, and the ensuing sorrow of grief. Oft times, if this is the first child for a young couple, their life's experiences have not prepared them for such a tragedy. This can complicate the grief experience even more. These parents need extra attention and direction through this uncharted experience upon which they are tragically embarking.

Losing a child to miscarriage is tragic. Statistics average that one-fourth of pregnancies end in miscarriage. To help a young couple recover from such a loss, one should offer recognition for their loss of life, and encourage open expression of grief.

25

SUDDEN DEATH

Grief is a painful and drawn out process, which every human being will at one time, or another experience. Each survivor must experience, suffer through and adjust to their unique grief experience. Those that do not, will find their suffering increase day after day, week after week, month after month and year after year, until they are unable to return to a life without depression and extreme pain by themselves. They will most likely require the intervention of professional counseling and possibly medication. One cannot avoid the grief experience, no matter how strongly they turn from it or deny it.

Grief is painful, especially when it is sudden or unanticipated. Sudden or unanticipated deaths include heart attacks, strokes, postoperative deaths, allergic reactions, sudden infant death as well as others. When grief is associated with sudden or unanticipated death, complicated grief is a viable reality. When death is sudden or unexpected, survivors will be ill prepared for the experiences that will follow. The lack of forewarning robs the mourner of appropriate time to anticipate and prepare for the grief that follows the passing of a significant loved one. Sudden, accidental, unexpected and traumatic death, shatters life, as we know it. These deaths do not make since, they are unfair and they leave us feeling shaken, insecure and vulnerable. Not only must we overcome the grief of our loss, we must also deal with the fear and insecurities of the impending changes that will most assuredly follow. Without forewarning, we will not have had ample time to process and prepare for these changes. The opportunity for developing alternative plans for continued obligations, such as rearing of children, college tuition for those children etc. will not have happened. Losses of income, loss of one's home and loss of social standing are viable concerns that will not have established recovery plans for the survivor.

The issues from sudden or unanticipated death, set the survivor up for an extended or complicated grief experience. In such circumstances, survivors will need extra support and understanding from family and friends. Support groups can be of some value, as well as spiritual foundations and counseling.

Traumatic deaths bring even more difficulties for the survivor. Traumatic deaths are those involving violence, mutilation, destruction, multiple deaths, random deaths and those where the survivor suffered near death. Traumatic deaths fit into the same category of sudden and unanticipated deaths however, recovery from this type of death is even more difficult and severe. Traumatic deaths bring fears and phobias that can be extremely extended, difficult to understand and require intense recovery techniques. Traumatic death fears and phobias can add recovery time and require more intense techniques, which the survivor may not be able to identify or understand without professional intervention. Often, traumatic deaths involve the justice system and social services will intervene and offer counseling for survivors that are under the age of accountability.

If you or someone you know or love has suffered a sudden, unanticipated or traumatic death, please seek out support systems to assist with coping and recovery from this terrifying and egregious experience. Due to the emotional and psychological trauma accompanying these categorically related deaths, the added stigma of victimization must be considered. Recovery perils may loom about creating problems the survivor might be ill equipped to surmount alone. In extreme cases, possible psychosis creates a strong argument for professional assistance before it presents itself.

26

GRIEF'S PHYSICAL PAIN

Grief manifests itself in many painful facets. There is emotional pain, psychological pain, spiritual pain, the pain of loneliness, the pain of sadness and even physical pain. Physical pain is very often brought on through continued avoidance of the grief experience.

Not everyone suffers the same amount or type of pain once a loved one dies. The pain intensity is usually predicated on the level of attachment the survivor experiences with the deceased. It is nearly impossible, however, to avoid a painful experience at the loss of someone with whom you shared an attachment. Of important note, the deceased need not be a loved one to feel pain at his or her passing.

When I was a young woman, I joined a large corporation in a secretarial capacity. It was not long after I began working there that one of the district managers died. Although I worked in a different office building, and had only seen this man at regional meetings, I was affected by his loss. My attachment to the company included this man as an integral part of my newly acquired associated network. I pondered my pain at his loss for many years, and truly did not understand it until I entered funeral service. Although, I did not know him very well at all, our work overlapped. I relied on his reports to compose my reports. I had an attachment to him because I had a reliance on his work. His passing created a structural defect in the security of my newly acquired income. The stress, though short lived, was very unnerving.

If grief is left unresolved or ignored, it will eventually surface in one's life as physical ailments. Grief shifts into medical conditions as an underlying cause. If you find that you are developing unexplained physical or mental conditions, you might discover that if you will address your grief issues, your other conditions might actually resolve themselves. Grief affects the body and soul the same way stress does. If you continue to ignore your grief, other conditions will develop that are avoidable by allowing the pain of grief to present itself and working through it.

I hope that if you have experienced unresolved grief that you will find the courage to face it and overcome the ill effects it creates within your physical and mental health. If you can muster up the courage to do it, you and those around you will benefit immensely. Your health will be better, and your life will be better too.

27

EMBALMING, A SCIENTIFIC PROCESS

Embalming is a scientific process that serves one purpose over its many others. That purpose is to prolong a decedent's presentational integrity.

As a funeral practitioner, I am often asked about embalming. Some clients want to know what it entails scientifically; some are spiritually concerned, while others have a morbid interest in the details.

"Except in certain special cases, embalming is not required by law..." (Federal Trade Commission (FTC), Funeral Rule, Disclosure No. 2) This statement begs the question, "What are the certain special cases and do they apply to my loved one?" Embalming is not required if a loved one is going to be cremated or buried without services, as in Direct Cremation or Immediate Burial. Services include viewings, visitations, funerals and graveside services where the body will be available for others to see. Without embalming, the body may not be present at any type of service where the public may be exposed to it. In some cases, a family may choose to have a visitation with a closed casket or a funeral with a closed casket, and in these cases, embalming may not be required.

Generally, without embalming, the service must take place within 24 hours of death. There are extenuating circumstances, however. If your loved one were brutally murdered and sent for autopsy, the funeral home would not have your loved one for a number of days. Quite often, brutal murders negate the opportunity for viewing due to extensive damage to the deceased, rendering the body unembalmable. The family may still have a visitation and funeral with the body present with the added services of refrigeration and Mylar encasement. Viewing, however will not be lawful or possible.

Embalming does not extend the decedent's presentational integrity indefinitely. Although decomposition has been chemically impeded, it has not been stopped; it merely continues to decompose on a slower schedule. How long the decedent's presentational integrity is preserved is dependent on a multitude of factors. The condition of the body at death, the illnesses suffered by the deceased and the span of time between death and embalming. In most cases, if the body is in good condition before embalming and if embalming takes place within a few hours of death, the decedent's presentational integrity is extended for three to five days. If additional time is required and your embalmer is pro-actively working on the body daily, eight days may be possible. In rare cases, if the embalmer is diligently exercising restorative measures, one might be able to press an additional day or two more.

Funeral Practitioners are trained in the arts of restoration, however, if a deceased individual was brutally murdered, even restoration may not be what the family wants to see. If you ever suffer such a tragic experience, discuss it as openly as possible with your funeral practitioner, they will be honest about the esthetic possibilities of the restorative work.

Embalming is required with any funeral that includes services where the casket may be opened. Other situations requiring embalming are those that require transportation of the body. In some states and counties across America, a body may not be transported across county or state borders without embalming. Air travel and dangerous or contagious diseases also require embalming.

28

DYING FROM A BROKEN HEART

Many have said, "She died of a broken heart." Seriously, is it possible to die from a broken heart?

Grief creates a mountain of stress and sorrow. Once we have lost a significant loved one, our world is suddenly no longer, as it was, and never will be again. The happiness, security and love we enjoyed yesterday have slipped away, and we are left to reconstruct our existence without the assistance and companionship of our loved one.

Studies show that, after one year of bereavement, 13% of survivors suffer from panic disorders and 39% suffer from anxiety. Of those suffering anxiety disorders, 55% also suffer from depression. Once a survivor enters into a state of depression, an open door invites other debilitating stressors to take root.

Grief should not be taken lightly. Some people might think, after a period of time, we should return to our normal selves. One hopes this is the case; however, not everyone passes through grief so smoothly. In fact, you may pass through one grief experience quite smoothly, yet suffer greatly from another.

When we think of grief, we associate depression as the culprit that interferes with our recovery. We should not, however, discredit the ravages of loneliness on one's ability to return to a healthy state of mind and physical health. Loneliness severely attacks the functionality of our immune system. If one already suffers from autoimmune disease, precautionary measures should be explored with their physician.

Persons suffering loneliness are more susceptible to increased inflammation in the body, atherosclerosis, learning and memory problems, higher rates of cancer, high blood pressure, heart attacks, strokes and viral invaders. (Biological Effects of Loneliness, Cacioppo)

Typical loneliness is experienced when one is temporarily isolated from what is normal and comfortable. An example of typical loneliness might be experienced when one begins a new job, starts college or moves to a new town. Typically, feelings of loneliness subside by themselves within six months or less. Loneliness associated with death is not typical. Death is not a temporary reality; it is a permanent one. When loneliness becomes chronic, it moves into isolation. Isolation negatively affects humans psychologically and physiologically. This affect can be severe, yet has a rather simple remedy.

In his study "Biological Effects of Loneliness," Cacioppo discovered that there are two profound methods for recovery from loneliness. The first is to retrain the survivor's social abilities and skills, and the second is to reintroduce them into social activities. It seems the less social we are, the more socially inept we become. Bringing people together to share good times should be familiar and comforting to the survivor. Small gatherings of close friends might be the best method of social reintroduction. As the survivor rediscovers the benefits of socialization and becomes stronger and more comfortable, small social gatherings will eventually graduate into social events.

If you find that someone you care for has become isolated after suffering the loss of a loved one, earnestly seek him or her out. A visit once each week will not kill you, but it might very well be the beginning of their recovery from life threatening isolation, and debilitating loneliness.

Is it possible to die from a broken heart? I believe it might be.

29

WHEN A LOVED ONE HAS BEEN MURDERED

When a loved one has been murdered, many difficulties arise for the survivors. Murder crosses into numerous death categories, all of which carry serious emotional and psychological obstacles to overcome. No matter who you are, if a significant loved one has been murdered, you will experience unparalleled grief. Murder falls into the traumatic death category, as well as unanticipated and sudden death categories. Sudden and unanticipated deaths are difficult from which to recover. Under these circumstances, the survivor has been robbed of ample time to set into motion, plans to compensate for their loss. Add to this, the experience of murder, and the survivor is destined to have a ruff go of the grief recovery process. Preparations for loss of income, loss of social standing and loss of companionship are losses that survivors can plan for if they have sufficient notice that a death is imminent. If the death is predictable, families can plan accordingly. A family planning to purchase a new and larger home might decide to stay put, once they know the household provider has a terminal illness. That same family, suffering the murder of the household provider and having recently purchased their dream home, may now be facing repossession of their home. These are unfair and unpredictable situations.

In addition to the suddenness of a murder, the violence experienced by the loved one is overwhelming. Details of the murder might be kept from the family in order to protect them and to protect the integrity of the investigation. The family might hear details that may or may not be accurate through the media. They might possibly see and hear additional details day after day, as the news replays and reports on the murder investigation. This experience can create a mountain of issues and setbacks for the survivors. If the murder is high profile, the family might not even be able to go out to dinner without overhearing conversations of speculation regarding their loved one's horrific experience. Speculation can be especially difficult for the family, as it is often inaccurate and cruel.

As years pass, the survivors of a brutal murder will be haunted by mental anguish. Try as they might, questions are always lingering in the backs of their minds. How long did their loved one suffer, were they frightened, did they call out for their family, how long did the brutality last, was death quick, were they humiliated before death, etc. Their questions are never completely answered, and so they must accept that they must live with the uncertainty of the suffering, sustained by their loved one. It is overwhelming and torturing to the survivors. In some instances, death may have been so brutal that the body of a loved one is non-viewable. If the family is unable to view the body, they are robbed of their final farewell. Survivors may question their belief in a deity and lose their way. They may become disillusioned with the justice system, especially if the murderer is not held accountable due to some legal technicality or mistake.

The fact of the matter is that murder is cruel and unjust. Survivors are going to suffer psychologically, the vicious actions of a demented human being upon their loved one. Emotional and psychological pathologies are going to plague the survivors for quite some time. Some survivors may never be able to accept that life continues and will be permanently held prisoner in the psychosis that follow.

As a funeral director, I have witnessed this tragedy upon families I have served. As a child, I witnessed my mother suffer this tragedy. Murder is a horrific perpetration. Unfortunately, it is one that is inflicted upon families throughout the world, daily.

If you have suffered the murder of a loved one, I extend my deepest condolences.

30

THE PAIN OF GRIEF

Grief manifests itself in many painful facets. There is emotional pain, psychological pain, spiritual pain, the pain of loneliness, the pain of sadness and even physical pain. Physical pain is very often brought on through continued avoidance of the grief experience.

Not everyone suffers the same amount or type of pain once a loved one dies. The pain intensity is usually predicated on the level of attachment the survivor experiences with the deceased. It is nearly impossible, however, to avoid a painful experience at the loss of someone with whom you shared an attachment. Of important note, the deceased need not be a loved one to feel pain at his or her passing.

When I was a young woman, I joined a large corporation in a secretarial capacity. It was not long after I began working there, that one of the district managers died. Although I worked in a different office building, and had only seen this man at regional meetings, I was affected by his loss. My attachment to the company included this man as an integral part of my newly acquired associated network. I pondered my pain at his loss for many years, and truly did not understand it until I entered funeral service. Although, I did not know him very well at all, our work overlapped. I relied on his reports to compose my own. I had an attachment to him because I had a reliance on his work. His passing created a structural defect in the security of my newly acquired income. The stress, though short lived, was very unnerving.

If grief is left unresolved or ignored, it will eventually surface in one's life as physical ailments. Grief shifts into medical conditions as an underlying cause. If you find that you are developing unexplained physical or mental conditions, you might discover that if you addressed your grief issues, your other conditions actually resolve themselves. Grief affects the body and soul the same way stress does. If you continue to ignore your grief, other conditions will develop that are avoidable by allowing the pain of grief to present itself and working through it.

I hope that if you have experienced unresolved grief, you will find the courage to face it and overcome the ill effects it creates within your physical and mental health. If you can muster up the courage to do it, you and those around you will benefit immensely. Your health will be better, and your life will be better too.

31

MISCARRIAGE RECOVERY

Generally, when a mother has miscarried, the first and immediate concern is her health. It is only later that others begin to realize that a life has been lost. The mother and father have immediate concern for future pregnancies, as well. Their grief may be postponed, relying on the possibility of a future pregnancy. If this is not the first born, the parents have the additional painful experience of helping their other children grieve the loss of their miscarried sibling.

Self-blame is another major issue for the parents of a miscarried pregnancy. The mother may blame herself for some activity, or her husband for his absence in protecting the integrity of the pregnancy. Generally, the father feels powerless through this tragedy. His confusion and helplessness may be misinterpreted by those around him as aloofness. While it is true that both mother and father grieve the loss of an unborn child, the longer the pregnancy, the more intense the grief, especially for the father.

Miscarriages involve the loss of a child's life. It is, therefore, paramount that parents experience and successfully accomplish grief work. Established rituals in our society to help parents experiencing the loss of an unborn child are virtually non-existent. There are, however, things one can do to help the grieving couple through their tragedy.

Naming the baby is of great value. A name gives the baby a tangible spot in the line of births within this family. It recognizes that there is another member of the family and reserves the sanctity for the child to be remembered and loved.

A memorial service offers an event for commemoration and solidifies the reality of the loss. This realism offers an opportunity for the parents and others to begin their grieving process. It marks a day for tradition, and gives dignity to the child that once existed within the mother's womb and in the family's wished-for future.

Planting a tree in the child's honor also helps with the healing process. As the years progress, the tree will grow. The parallel symbolism helps the parents and any siblings of the child cope with the passing years.

Some families find a journal helps with grief. A journal for all members of the family to write special moments and wishes for the miscarried child, helps to solidify the structure of the family, and the child's place within the family.

Some parents choose to bury their child. Burying the child gives the family a place to visit and includes the child as a legitimate member of their family. This is especially helpful to younger children. It helps them understand that their sibling had value, that he or she was loved, and gives them confidence that they are loved and valued, as well.

The miscarriage of a child is tragic. However, with the love of family and friends, grief recovery is possible for the devastated mother, father and siblings if any.

32

ST. PATTY'S DAY

In 2009, over one-third of all car accidents that occurred in the US on Saint Patrick's Day involved alcohol. These accidents resulted in nearly 50 deaths.

When I was an intern for my professional license, it occurred to me that a good number of Americans choose the way they will die. They do this through the various choices, activities or habits they incorporate into their lives. Unfortunately, when these choices have fatal consequences, there are innocent victims who suffer these senseless losses. The fact remains, if you want to avoid injury or potential death, certain holidays tend to be more dangerous than others.

As a funeral practitioner, I have seen deaths caused by any manner of poor judgment and excessive risk. I find, however, more often than not, this type of death involves alcohol over any other faculty altering substance. The pain suffered by the survivors of a loved one, who has senselessly lost his or her life over the holiday weekend, is sad indeed.

During the development of my funeral director persona, I adopted a new habit. When I see someone doing something excessively risky, I walk up to them and offer my business card. As they reach to take it, I ask them to save it in their wallet, as I am sure they will need my services in the near future. If the person is an obvious minor, I ask them to give my card to their parent. It is a shocking experience for the recipient. If they have not previously recognized the danger in which they have put themselves, they generally do at this point. My goal is to help save lives. If my actions help save even one life, it is worth the interesting reactions and comments I receive.

With Saint Patrick's Day upon us, I plead with you to take the necessary precautions to avoid being that guy or gal in your state, that becomes the St. Patty's Day statistic. If you are going out with a group of friends and know you will be drinking, please designate a sober driver or utilize the designated driver program, www.drinkinganddriving.org/designated-driver-services/. Another option is to call a taxi and retrieve your vehicle once the effects of alcohol have subsided. If your party is at a hotel or within walking distance of a hotel, perhaps you and your party friends could arrange for overnight accommodations at the hotel. The following morning you might enjoy breakfast together before returning to your individual homes. If all else fails, call mom and dad. As a parent of adult children, I would be more than happy to rescue them from themselves, should the need ever arise. One last suggestion, just stay home.

Remember, just because the holiday is dangerous, does not mean that you must live dangerously. There are simple precautions you can take to ensure that your holiday is a little safer than it was last year. As a funeral director/embalmer, I assure you, I would prefer seeing you on my table when you are 91 rather than 19.

Enjoy your holiday.

33

HIDDEN TREASURE

When I was a young girl, I loved scavenger hunts. At a party, I would receive a list of ordinary things to collect from neighbors homes, along with one or two not so ordinary things. The party host would divide the partygoers into small groups and off we would go on our own little treasure hunt. Once we had collected all of the items; or, at the appointed time if we had not collected every item, we would return to the party home and compare treasures. It was a very fun game filled with thrills of treasure seeking.

As an adult, I have a daughter who loves scavenger hunts of a different nature. She is a teenage Genealogist sleuth. She combs the internet, lists, books, old letters, documents and any other thing she can put her hands on, seeking information on our ancestral lineage. When she finds her treasure, she is filled with excitement and happiness. I have seen her diligently search for one bit of information for years on end, meeting one disappointment after another. She remains ever conscientious though, knowing that if she remains focused and ever hopeful, her search will find success. She has much more faith in the process than I.

When I was an intern for my professional license, I worked at a very old funeral home in Dallas, TX. The building was huge and had those six feet wide columns across the front porch. One day at work, I set about clearing out an old bookcase upon which sat a large collection of lovely leather bound books. I would estimate that there were at least 40 of these books on the shelves. They were very old, and some were showing signs of deterioration. I asked the Funeral Director in Charge (FDIC) what he would have me do with these old, dusty, musty smelling, leather bound books. He said, "Just through them away; I don't know why we have them." His remarks startled me, and I have never forgotten them. These old leather bound books dating back to the 1800's were hand written ledgers, containing the vital statistics and personal impressions of the FDIC of every person this funeral home had buried for over 100 years. Can you imagine coming across such a trove of hidden information?

My mother was a genealogist. Perhaps that is where my daughter inherits such passion for her skill. I remember my mother taking trips to the Deep South to visit old cathedrals in search for lost information in her family lineage. Instead of spending our summers as our friends did, on the coast or at amusement parks, my siblings and I were packed into my mother's station wagon to visit old relatives and catholic priests all summer. We would return to our home just in time for school to begin. Each day after school, we would sit and work on our studies. My mother would sit at the dining room table with us. She would comb through her newly acquired documents in search for illusive ancestral linkage. She, like my daughter, would revel when she would find her bits of hidden treasure.

While writing this story this morning, I have placed a phone call to the old funeral home in Dallas where I interned. The secretary has not yet arrived at work, so I have left a message for her. I pray those old leather bound books filled with lost treasure have not been destroyed as the FDIC suggested. I hope to rescue them and digitize them so that if there is a genealogist out there searching for a lost member of their family, they might find their treasure through my efforts.

Before becoming a funeral practitioner, I did not know about these books. My mother would have jumped for joy if she had ever come across such a hidden treasure. I hope that if you are searching for lost genealogical records, this information might help you find your lost loved ones.

When I was a young girl, I loved scavenger hunts. Gone are the days that I searched for common items. I am now embarking on a hunt for hidden genealogical treasure, and mortuaries are my oyster.

34

KITTY

Before I became a funeral director, I had a dear friend who lost her adult son to cancer. I had been out of town working for quite some time, and when I returned to the intermountain west, in the dead of winter, I met with her at a restaurant for hot cocoa. My friend was a highly respected and accomplished woman. She had been the state president of a nationwide political organization and worked for very important men. She was strong and very intelligent. I had worked beside my friend for many years and was very sad to learn that during my absence, she had lost her son.

Once we were seated, we ordered our cocoa and my dear friend began telling me about the death of her son. Her son resided in a coastal state and had returned home to live with his parents, as he passed through the final year of his life. As she began telling me about his journey to death, she would naturally cry. When she came to a particularly difficult moment, she would pause and look at me. I was just crying away without regard to other patrons in the restaurant. During one pause, she reached out and took my hand in hers. After looking deep into my soul, she said something to me.

At the time, I thought it was a very important statement. It struck me deeply, and I pondered it for a long time. As a funeral director, I have often reflected back on this experience with my friend, and I have realized that she shared something profound with me. Throughout my days as a funeral director, I have shared this "Pearl of Wisdom" with many of my clients.

Her enlightening words were these. "Thank you for letting me tell you the story of my son's death. It seems that each time I tell someone about his death, it erases some of my sadness."

We sat at the restaurant and cried together as she finished telling the story of her son's death. I left with tear stained cheeks, and my friend left a little less devastated.

You see, that is what death does. It devastates us. When we experience the death of someone we love, we are devastated. If you learn only one thing from this article, if you cannot bear one more moment of the overwhelming sadness that accompanies significant loss, listen and learn from the profound words of my dear friend.

Tell your story. Share it with everyone who will listen. Telling your story helps take your sadness away. It helps you to realize and accept the death of your loved one. Once you have accomplished this necessary realization, you are free to recover, and you will learn how to live life without your loved one with you.

This is the greatest thing you can do for your grief recovery.

35

MISSING TODDLER

When my daughter was a toddler, my husband served in the US Navy, and we lived in a very large coastal California city. One day my husband and I decided, for entertainment, we would like to go to a large swap meet. We loaded up our toddler, invited my mother and away we went. It was a wonderful activity, filled with exciting things to see and purchase. The prices were low and the local delicacies abundant. We were having a fabulous time.

About two hours into our activity, I walked over to my husband, who was shopping a different booth than I, and noticed that our toddler was not in her stroller. I asked my husband where she was, thinking that my mother must have her, and my husband said, "She's in her stroller." Suddenly, my whole life changed. My wonderful day of pleasure shopping abruptly changed into a horrid emergent situation. I felt as though I could not breathe, it seemed as if the world began to spin a million miles per minute. My toddler was missing at an open-air swap meet, in a large and dangerous city, and I had no idea where she was or what might be happening to her.

My husband, being the organizer that he is, immediately sprang into action. He instantly located my mother and sent her to the business office to alert security. Her next task was to go to the entry gate and detain anyone trying to exit with a child near the age of our daughter. My husband headed toward the restrooms to inspect them for our daughter or signs of foul play, and I was to comb through the rows and rows of shopping booths, calling out my daughter's name and scanning for anyone that might be trying to escape with her. We all three sprang into our appointed duties. I ran as fast as a cheetah, calling my daughter's name and inspecting anyone and everyone within the isles and shops. I was frantic, just recalling the event, is causing my heart to race slightly and my eyes to tear. As I rounded a corner, I saw a woman, tugging my daughter by the hand. My child was hysterical and I am sure I looked a fright, because the woman quickly threw her hands up in the air and started yelling that she had found my daughter and was taking her to security.

Sobbing, I fell to my knees and held my child tightly to my chest. My daughter was equally distraught; she was crying and holding onto me just as tightly. Oh my, I cannot tell you what a horrid experience that was. I had felt as if my life were over. Lost in a whirlwind of panic and fear. I had felt unbelievable anguish and inconceivable despair. We left the swap meet and went directly to a large warehouse, where we purchased a personal alarm for my daughter. She has never been lost again.

Many times over the years, as I have watched her grow into a wonderful woman, (currently expecting her own child), I have reflected back on that horrific experience. The thought of what could have happened to her that day, still frightens me and almost brings me to my knees. If my daughter had been kidnapped that day or killed, I do not know that I could have lived on without her. The pain, anguish and self-blame would have been too much to bear. I am so thankful that she was all right, that I found her and that the poor woman who had her was a Good Samaritan, rather than a demented crazy axe murderer. My experience although terribly frightening ended with a positive resolution.

The feelings and panic I experienced that dreadful day were real and powerful. They pale, however, in comparison to those a family feels, when they have unexpectedly lost a loved one. Unexpected loss brings a multitude of issues beyond those of an anticipated loss. When a loved one has been ill, or has been suffering severe pain for an extended time, although we mourn the loss, death is sometimes a relief for those witnessing, day in and day out, the unrelenting pain and suffering of their family member or close friend. When death is unexpected or sudden, family and close friends develop regrets, they are robbed of the time they need to prepare themselves psychologically, as well as time for resolving any unfinished business or issues existing between themselves and the deceased. These issues will fester over time and can become severe health issues, both psychologically and physically.

Equally robbed is their opportunity to simply say "good-bye." This simple moment, shared between those we love, is immensely important. Being robbed of this final rite creates a helplessness that is difficult to overcome. Mourners may carry this pain with them for a very long time, and some are unable to overcome it. Pair with this the regret of unfinished business, the anguish of a brutal death, or the eternal yearning for an unfound loved one, and a recipe for extreme extension with a myriad of additional complications to overcome, for the accomplishment of grief recovery develops.

Currently in the news, one intently follows the disappearance of the commercial 777 jetliner. The sorrow on the faces, and behavior of the families suffering through this crisis, reveal these complications. These families need extreme support and aggressive counseling, rather than being abruptly escorted away from those who should be offering insights and answers. With leadership comes great responsibility. With the absence of information and answers, responsible leaders should render greater latitude and understanding, than is being offered to these families in despair. We continue to hope for the safe return of the commercial 777 jetliner and it's passengers. We know that their families do too. In the end, if this is not realized, we hope and pray for their recovery. These families may indeed be forced to begin their road to recovery without resolution.

Although unlikely, my fervent prayer is that these unfortunate families with loved ones aboard the 777 jetliner would have the same resolution of having their loved ones returned to them whole and unharmed, as I did with my toddler. In that this scenario is less and less probable as the days painfully pass, I pray that the world and especially those in authoritative roles, will render them the tender consideration and extended grief care resources, of which they so desperately stand in need.

36

CHOOSE RECOVERY

I visited with a mother last week, who had suffered financially and emotionally at the hands of her recently deceased son. She vocalized her anger toward her son and her disappointment in herself for these feelings. Upon further discussion, I discovered that her son had suffered a severe drug addiction and had involved himself in activities that were quite dangerous. His exploitation of his mother has left her nearly destitute, and she is suffering financial consequences as well as the intense grief that follows the loss of a child (even when the child is an adult at death).

Where does she go from here? Her grief is overwhelming. Her son is now deceased. She feels as though her sacrifices for him were for naught. The financial crisis in which she now finds herself only exacerbates her grief. What then is she to do, to rectify this situation and move forward in her grief recovery? Her goal is to be able to mourn the loss of her son with fond memories and love, rather than pain and resentment. She is in a tough situation indeed. The financial pressure of making ends meet is interfering with her ability to move from resentment into grief recovery. Unfortunately, her son committed suicide shortly after a realistic conversation between the two of them, addressing the severe consequences of his situation. This conversation and his self-infliction of death compound her sadness, regret and confusion.

How then do we help this heartbroken mother recover from this tragic situation? How do we help her mend her feelings of guilt, resentment, anger, panic and embarrassment? Fortunately, she is willing to discuss her feelings. This indicates that she is desirous of resolution. She is hopeful yet lost; confused on what to do or where to go for help in her recovery journey.

The first step toward recovery is to choose to recover. She has made that decision. The second step is to move forward with recovery. How does one accomplish this? The easiest way to recover from a tragedy is to have someone support you and help keep you focused. This mother has a second adult child, who is mourning the loss of her sibling, yet is willing and actively involved in supporting her mother through this journey. After meeting with the both of them, I am confident that they are moving toward resolution and that together, although their road will be bumpy and filled with potholes of despair, they will eventually arrive at their destination of peace.

The mother will suffer through the financial stress of debt recovery, but she will realize that her sacrifices were out of unconditional love for her son. Although she will have internal regrets that her financial support may have enabled him to continue his destructive behavior and eventual fatal demise, she will realize that her funds were merely a way of keeping him close, allowing her to affect his choices in a more positive direction. She will eventually understand that her last conversation with him was not abandonment; it was encouragement to reach his potential by letting go of a life that was filled with danger and evil.

I visited with a mother last week, who had suffered greatly at the hands of her deceased son. I discovered that she was a great mother who loved her son deeply, a mother who had sacrificed all that she had to save her son, and now was left with the unimaginable sorrow of losing her son to drug induced suicide. A desperate and tragic situation at best. More importantly though, I discovered that this tragic loss was serving to bring a mother and daughter closer together. I witnessed two women in tragedy bond together. Each helping the other overcome the great sorrows that come with extreme tragedy. I saw them choose to embark on recovery rather than tragedy.

I saw the moment their recovery began.

37

MAN OF STEEL

My first case as a fully licensed funeral practitioner was my Uncle Roy Don Zylks. As I was sitting in church Easter Sunday, I was reminiscing over family gatherings and events I had shared with my Uncle Roy Don. He was the strongest man I had ever known. He could pull the engine out of a car without the assistance of a lifting winch. He had super strength; he was a "Man of Steel." He had grown up in a rougher time, when people worked hard for what they had and fought hard to keep it. Men would come from far and wide to challenge his strength. They always left with a new respect for his reputation. I had seen him do so many things in life that were physically impossible for the average person. His super strength is what had kept him going after losing his beloved, Betty Jean. I prayed for him that day at church. Prayed that he would have the strength to live another day, so that my cousins would not lose their father on Easter.

As church was ending, my cell phone rang. I walked out into the foyer to answer it, and my cousin informed me that her father had just passed away. Now every year when Easter comes around, I think of my Uncle Roy Don and the special experiences I shared with him when he was living. I see my cousins, his daughters, either around town or on social media, and every year at Easter, they express memories of their late father.

When one has lost a significant loved one on a holiday, that holiday instantly changes forever in their heart. The primary focus or celebration now becomes the marker in one's memory, as the day they suffered the loss of their loved one. The first few years, one may be sad when that holiday comes around. One hopes that the sadness of the death experience will eventually be replaced with happy memories of wonderful times shared together. Reality however, works at a snail's pace, and such a change does not happen quickly.

One need not lose a loved one on a holiday to feel an increase of pain on holidays. The loneliness of loss is magnified every holiday, as we cycle through the first year, and each year after a substantial loss. Holidays are set aside for family and close friend gatherings. They are social events, shared with those we love most. By disrupting our social circles, death disrupts our social events. If you know someone who has lost a loved one, be mindful that he or she might delight in a thoughtful card, call or visit to get through a very painful day.

I was so honored that my cousins called upon me to lay their beloved father to rest. It shall remain forever a special memory, that they put their trust in me to get them through such a dreadful experience. Moreover, Easter has forever changed for me. The profound celebration depicting the resurrection of our Savior gives me hope that one day, my darling cousins will reunite with their real life superhero, "Man of Steel."

38

THE OBIT

Occasionally, I work with a family wishing to forgo the printing of the death announcement, a.k.a. obituary, in the newspaper. Before becoming a funeral practitioner, I, as these families, thought obituaries unnecessary and a bit obsolete, especially if the decedent's circles of friends and family were small. I have a rather small group of immediate and intimate friends and family, and have thought in the past, that when my time comes, the printing of an obituary would be unnecessary. After becoming a funeral director and working with families for a few years, my opinion of the necessity of an obituary notice, printed in the newspaper, has most definitely changed. It is a small bit of money, very well spent.

A death notice, a.k.a. obituary is a quick and fairly inexpensive way of notifying the living, that an acquaintance, friend, relative, co-worker, etc. has recently died. It also informs them of the service dates and times if they wish to attend or send condolences.

The obituary lists the names of family who have preceded the decedent in death, as well as the survivors. This is a very important part of the obituary. Listing the preceding kinship and surviving kinship allows readers to recognize those in their community that will be entering bereavement. It also allows them to link families and verify that they may, or may not know the decedent. This knowledge also allows the community to understand the unusual melancholy behavior among the survivors with greater understanding and compassion.

The obituary may also be used by HR services, to verify and allow bereavement leave for family members. It also verifies time off for staff and personnel wishing to attend services. On occasion, it may be used for certain bereavement allowances and discounts.

The most important role of the obituary, however, is to link genealogy. The listing of kindred dead and living survivors serves as a printed witness for family historians and genealogists. Obituaries can be used as evidentiary paperwork to prove lineage when other documents are not available. The obituary lists personality characteristics of the decedent, as well. This information is a treasure trove for the generations that follow. Saving and re-reading obituaries may bring comfort and serve as therapeutic grief recovery tools in the months and years that follow a significant loss.

If you have suffered the loss of a loved one or expect a loss in the future, please consider the importance of a well-written obituary. I have researched loved ones through obituaries. If fortune is smiling upon me, there will be a picture included. These tiny bits of genealogical treasure bring me great joy.

39

THE ARRANGEMENT CONFERENCE

As I was ordering lunch at a local fast food restaurant, my cell phone rang. I stepped to the side and answered the call. It was my three o'clock appointment. He said that he had come by early and was sitting in front of my funeral home with his mother. I canceled my order and returned to my office.

As I parked my car, I saw his mother first. She was a beautiful woman, tall with striking silver hair. She was dressed in purple, and it suited her. As we greeted, I looked deep into her eyes, from the depth of her soul, she radiated gentleness and kindheartedness.

Her son was exiting their car. As I turned my attention toward him, I noticed that although he was young, his movements were measured with caution. As he rose, I could see that he, as his mother, stood tall. He matched her beauty, both inwardly and outwardly. He was remarkably handsome and radiated a tranquility one does not often witness in young adult men.

They were both friendly, and I invited them into my funeral home. As we walked the first twenty feet or so, I could see the young man's strength waiver. He immediately sought out a couch and sat down. His mother and I spoke for another few moments, and then I invited them into my arrangement room. I immediately offered each of them a General Price Sheet and began narrowing their needs.

The handsome young man asked about various funeral options, and as he began to make choices, a tear or two would spill out of the corner of his eye. He would immediately brush it away, perhaps pause for a moment, regain his composure and continue with his arrangements. For a brief moment, he excused himself from the room. I could hear him in the hallway. He was very ill. I was overcome with respect and love for this young man and his mother. I looked at her. She sat there silent and still, listening to her son, as he struggled to catch his breath and regain his strength. I could see the worry and fear in her countenance. A tear or two spilled out of the corner of her eye as she struggled to maintain her composure. Her eyes met mine; they were wide and fearful. She excused herself and went into the hall to shore up her son.

As I listened to her encourage him, she emptied her heart with tenderness. Her expressions were the deepest love of a mother, witnessing the premature and painful death of her young adult child. I was overwhelmed with heartache for them. The reverence and pain of the moment was a heavy burden to witness.

I do not know what disease he suffers, only that it will take his life in the near future. A handsome young man in the prime of his life is losing his life, before his loving mother's eyes. For those few brief moments that I shared with them, I witnessed the unconditional love and excruciating heartache of a mother for her dying child. I could see in her eyes, and witness in her soul, that she would take his burden and trade his suffering for her health. If it were possible, she would gladly die in his place.

We completed his arrangements. He wanted it all written down and signed. His final act of strength was to lift this burden from his mother on the day she will suffer the most tremendous heartache known to mothers, the day of her beloved son's death, his death.

40

STILETTO JO

Last week was a great week for me. I received a call for help from a dear friend, whose mother had just passed away. I am a funeral director, and helping others when they are hurt to their core, when waking and functioning are more than they can bear, and when their lives have become bitterly painful, gives me great satisfaction.

I immediately drove my hearse over to my friend's house, which is just down the street from my own, and sat with her, holding her hand as she called and notified her family of their great loss. My friend is a brave woman. She is a therapist; her job is to help others heal. Healing others comes naturally to her, and she is great at it. She finds the good in people and helps them draw upon their inner strength for recovery. She is an amazing woman.

As I sat there, beside her, holding her hand, I felt her breath quiver and her hand tremble ever so slightly. I knew I was witnessing the courage of a healer, mustering all of the valor she held in reserve, for this most dreaded and grievous moment. She had just lost her mother, yet she was nurturing and comforting her own adult children through the heart wrenching realization of losing their beloved grandmother. It was a profound moment for me, because I saw her mother's matriarchal mantel pass onto her own capable shoulders.

Preparing my friend's mother for burial was an honor. I could see the ravages of her illness on her tiny body. I also saw the care and love my friend had rendered her mother, over the long and painful course of her disease. As brutal as Alzheimer's is on one's mind, it is likewise brutal on one's body. The years and months of confusion can be debilitating and dangerous on the patient, as well as their family. My friend had taken such loving care of her mother, that the usual physical signs of prolonged dying were absent from her mother's tiny body.

My friend brought her mother's clothing to me and along with the beautiful dress that her mother would wear when being laid to rest, was a pair of the loveliest stiletto heels. My friend had taken such meticulous care of her mother, that even her feet were beautifully manicured and in perfect health. My husband lifted my friend's mother in his arms, and cradled her as he carried her to her casket. When she lay there, I looked at her and thought, what a wonderful mother she must have been to have raised such an outstanding daughter. One that would become a healer and care for her in her final days.

Last week was a great week for me. I served a dear friend at the loss of her beloved mother. My reward was being able to witness the best in humanity at the most painful moment in life, the death of a treasured loved one.

I love my friend. I pray for her recovery, and I give thanks for my privilege in knowing her and serving her.

41

THE UN-DEAD

Recently, I have noticed a long list of movies, books and television series' that focus on the un-dead, the living dead or the zombie pseudo dead. As I have watched these topically based productions, I have been intrigued by the similarities of these half dead/half living persons compared to a survivor who is caught in a continual cycle of debilitating grief.

When a person is caught in a cycle of grief that continues for an extended period, we say that he or she is experiencing "complicated grief." In other words, the grief cycle seems to have trapped him or her, significantly retarding their recovery time table and negatively affecting their ability to re-enter normal functionality.

One wonders why one individual over another, finds him or herself unable to recover from a loss and exit the grief experience. Quite possibly, one does not ever recover completely from the loss of someone they love. They simply adjust their life's existence, enabling them to survive without the debilitating ache that finds its way into their hearts once loss has occurred.

Generally, when one finds him or herself in this extended state of grief, we recommend that they enter grief counseling or in extreme cases, psychotherapy. The advantages of counseling or therapy are that the professional grief advocate can intervene, and help the survivor identify habits that have trapped him or her into this undesirable state of non-recovery. This undesirable psychological state seems to hold these unfortunate survivors hostage as the un-dead, a state of mind where they exist, but they do not experience. Prolonged existence such as this will eventually land the grief stricken person into a state of serious depression and eventually psychosis. At this juncture, the depressed individual truly needs and should benefit from psychotherapy.

A qualified psychotherapist can help the grief-trapped individual identify habits and cycles of behavior that are inconducive to grief recovery. The counselor or psychotherapist can set into practice a positive growth experience; possibly yielding a sound recovery plan, that the survivor has been unable to identify, or obtain on his or her own. If the survivor has been trapped in this cycle for years on end, recovery may be a slow and complicated process. Their psychotherapist may utilize the benefits of prescription therapy to enable and enhance the recovery process.

If you find you have a friend or loved one trapped in the zombie pseudo experience of complicated grief, love and understanding may not have been enough to help them recover. It may be time to suggest something more substantial for their grief experience. Grief counseling or psychotherapy may be of great benefit to them.

42

GRIEF DESIGNATED AS DISORDER

According to the Los Angeles Times, the Diagnostic and Statistical Manual of Mental Disorders (DSM-V) recently added prolonged (complicated) grief disorder as an official psychiatric diagnosis, giving people who suffer from debilitating grief a name for the disorder. What does this mean for the poor soul suffering this excruciating disorder? It means that they can now identify their disorder by name, and seek out medical and psychiatric assistance for recovery.

In the past, survivors suffering debilitating grief were basically on their own to find a remedy and recover from their disorder. The work place is not obligated to accommodate grief recovery, only bereavement leave. It has been my experience that the work place has generally accepted two to three days as an appropriate time for bereavement leave. This slight recognition ignores the emotional affects of loss, and does not allow additional time to recover from the deep emotional and psychological trauma that comes with such a catastrophic experience.

If you break your limb and your doctor casts it, there is physical evidence that something is wrong. Your doctor might also send a note to your employer requiring that you receive a prescribed time of light duty or time off completely. In these cases, there is no question; your work is going to accommodate your needs during this time.

If your spouse or child suffers an accident severe enough to take his or her life, your employer may give you 2 to 3 days off work for funeral services. Unfortunately, they expect you back; bright eyed and bushy tailed as soon as the gravedigger covers up your loved one with earth. Fulfilling the customary ritual within our society, your co-workers and company of employment may send words and flowers of condolences for the services. The problem comes into play, when they fail to realize that although your loved one lost his or her life, you have lost your loved one. The wound to your soul, although invisible, is greater and more significant than any physical wound you will ever suffer. It appears that if your wounds are without outward marks of trauma, they are unrecognized as noteworthy. Perhaps with this new designation from the DSM, recognition is on the cusp of change.

As a funeral practitioner, I have seen a significant number of my clients; lose their jobs because they could not bring themselves to return to work after only 3 days of bereavement leave. These clients suffered significant losses of either their spouse or their child. Losses one would naturally expect would take more than three days from which to recover. The Family Medical Leave Act (FMLA) established in 1993, provides for up to 12 weeks unpaid leave per year for employees to address serious health conditions, care for a newborn or adopted child, recovery from illness, or care for a sick family member. It fails to recognize even one day for recovery from familial loss.

Familial loss inflicts a severe wound to one's soul. The psychological effects of such trauma can be devastating, and if left untreated or unresolved, may progress into a debilitating illness. The ensuing illness may manifest itself in mental and/or physical ailments. At this juncture, the FMLA may become applicable, as the survivor potentially qualifies for leave under personal serious illness. Isn't it sad, however, that survivors suffer grief to such a serious level, when it could have been treated early on, possibly preventing other illnesses from manifesting themselves. Even with treatment to these new illnesses, the underlying cause remains unaddressed and may, therefore, continue to cause poor and degenerating health.

During the Victorian Era, families wore black for one full year after the loss of a significant loved one. In so doing, they were notifying others that they were in a state of grief, that they would be functioning at a lower than anticipated level of competency, that they might be inexplicably melancholy and that they might require kindness and consideration during their daily activities and responsibilities. The Victorians automatically allowed considerations for the bereaved, yet in modern society, we barely recognize it as significant. Perhaps the identification of "Prolonged Grief Disorder" by the DSM will bring new awareness, research, recognition and treatment for those who suffer the catastrophic effects of complicated grief.

43

MEMORIAL DAY

A few weeks ago, my husband and I were out of town, dining at a country style restaurant. As our dinner was being prepared, we met a chief staff member from an elected U. S. Congressman's office. My husband engaged the staff member in conversation and inquired, to which Memorial Day ceremony would the staff member and Congressman attend in their district. The staff member informed us that the Congressman sees no reason to return from Washington DC to his area for such an event, and that he, the Congressman's chief representative, spends his Memorial Days at the lake.

Ordinarily, this would not offend me as I enjoy holidays, and I enjoy the lake. Memorial Day, however, is one of America's most observed holidays. It is one day out of 365 that Americans set aside to honor those who have given the ultimate sacrifice, while protecting our freedom. It is one of our most important holidays, as statistically, nearly every American has had a member of their family, serve our nation through one war, or another. I am a member of multiple organizations whose missions are to preserve the history, honor and graves of our fallen soldiers and deceased veterans from the beginning of our nation's history to the present. I have willingly taken this obligation, in order to honor my veteran kindred dead, as well as other veterans whose families are unable to attend their graves. Likewise, I engage in these organizations to educate my children and grandchildren of the life's blood their ancestors have shed, for the establishment and preservation of their rights, liberties and freedom.

As a funeral director, I serve mournful families as they lose their veterans. These honorable men and women deserve the love and appreciation of a grateful nation, as well as from their elected politicians. We do not observe military honors at these funerals simply to show off, we observe them out of reverence and respect for the veteran's selfless sacrifices on our behalf. Service members risk their lives and the well-being of their families to protect our nation's honor and freedom. They spend months and even years on unaccompanied tours in harm's way, so that we can go to the store and not fear a grenade exploding as we enter. It is inconceivable that a U. S. Congressman does not see the need to return to his district to honor the veterans he represents, or that his chief staff member would not see the importance of observing with reverence the sacrifices of our nation's veterans at a Memorial Day ceremony in the Congressman's unpardonable absence.

My husband is a military veteran. I am a military veteran's wife. I hold dear his honor and sacrifice to our nation. I hold dear the honor and sacrifice of each and every one of our nation's military veterans. I am saddened that Washington DC harbors elected politicians who do not understand or appreciate the sacrifices of our brave service members and their families. I love my country, and I respectfully serve families who are laying their beloved men and women of merit and honor to rest. It is my privilege to serve these families and help them through the worst day of their lives; the day they must say their final farewells and accept Old Glory as a token of appreciation from a grateful nation.

44

TROPHIES FOR EVERYONE

Reality is not candy; life is not always sweet.

In the funeral business, we see as time progresses, generations are less able to deal with the reality of death than their predecessors. In my opinion, the practice of "Everybody gets a trophy," plays into the lack of preparation and inability to deal with life's issues.

When we are children, our parents enroll us in activities to teach us life's lessons. One plays ball to learn good sportsmanship. In order to learn good sportsmanship, one must, at one time or another, lose the game. The disappointment of not winning helps us learn and appreciate the value of good solid preparation. We eventually grow to understand that the other team prepared better and played better than did we. Additionally, we grow to understand that these principles must be applied to ourselves if we ever wish to win the coveted trophy. This experience creates new resolve and greater motivation to do better, to prepare better and to work harder. It develops character in our children and teaches them how to adjust to the pain of losing. They learn to overcome adversity and disappointment, and in turn, they become dedicated human beings. In short, they have learned good sportsmanship, and it's by product, good stewardship. Their human nature has been tempered by the experience, and they have become stronger and better participants in the human race.

These small disappointments in childhood, prepare our children for larger disappointments as adults, and life in general. Losing games as a child helps one handle the stress and disappointment of losing a job as a teenager. In turn, this prepares one for the betrayal of a sweetheart in college, which may serve to prepare one for the responsibilities of adulthood. We hope these experiences will give us the wherewithal to cope with the many losses we will experience and endure, as we travel through life. One of these losses will be the loss of valued and loved friends and family members. Without the childhood experiences of losing games and not winning trophies, one will remain ill prepared for life's future disappointments, failures and opportunities for growth.

When we shield our children from pain, they grow up as mal-adjusted, soft adults. They are then, poorly prepared for what life will dole out to them. We set them up for complications in coping with disappointments, stress and eventually our deaths. In trying to protect them from pain, we set them up to experience the ultimate pain without any experience upon which to draw. Without these essential pain experiences as they travel through life, our children are unable to process the anxiety, fear and despair, which accompany the quintessential pain of all, bereavement.

The death of a loved one changes our identity, our social standing, our support structure, possibly our income, as well as a truckload of other issues. If our resolve is experienced and tempered through baby steps of loss and pain, we will be better prepared to face the worst times of our lives armed with the ability to overcome adversity and grief.

Reality is not candy; life will not always be sweet. Prepare your children for the knocks and bruises that life will through their way, by allowing them to experience small disappointments and failures without trophies. In so doing, you will have prepared them to withstand the most adverse experience known to man; the experience of losing a loved one, the experience of losing you.

45

I LOVE DAD

I am a member of a very large family and found this sweet paragraph on the internet, written by one of my dear cousins.

"My sweet little Daddy's happy birthday! So happy he is with Mother and all those he loves so much who have gone on. Nevertheless, I miss him so much and wish we could have one of our big heart to hearts! He taught me more riding along with him as we went to take care of the cows, hauling hay, going to the sale barn or just riding to town to get a so dee pop! Loved how he loved Memaw (his mother) and how he interacted with her. Loved how he lit up when he was around his siblings. Loved how devoted he was to Heavenly Father and his quiet devotion. He was amazing. I love him so much and still can't bear that he's gone!"

She continues, "Today, I fight back the tears that are so close to my heart as I miss my sweet little Daddy. I loved him so much."

My cousin's father was a wonderful man and meant so much to so many. Her tears are not a sign of weakness, they testify that the love and time she spent with her father were, and continue to be, a great treasure.

Eventually there will come a time when holidays and special events will be easier to manage, but one never forgets their father, nor the love they shared together; nor would you want to. Just because a loved one dies, does not mean that love has died too.

The heart wrenching pain expressed by my cousin, can sometimes be softened by developing new traditions based on old ones shared with the deceased. In my cousin's little paragraph, she mentioned that she had learned so much from her father while participating in his work, caring for his cattle, hauling hay and accompanying him to the sale barn. Now that her parents are deceased, she can develop these same special moments with her children and grandchildren by following her father's example. The death of a close loved one creates a wonderful opportunity to concentrate on developing those fabulous nuances that have created and molded you into the person you are today. Honor your father by passing on his greatest parenting skill or grand parenting skill. This would truly be a great compliment to your deceased loved one and an honor to his memory and accomplishments.

If you have the opportunity, please take this Father's Day to openly express your love for your dad before it is too late. In my line of work, I have seen young fathers as well as old, slip away without any warning, and at those times, I realize how utterly important it is to express your love and appreciation for all those you love, each and every moment you have with them.

Fathers are so important to the welfare and health of the family. They play an important role in their children's development into healthy functioning adults. As I see families pass through my funeral home, I can immediately recognize families blessed with a strong father, from those who were not. When parents die, realization of our own mortality, and the importance of being a strong and responsible parent, comes to the forefront of our minds. We vow to do better and regret our past shortcomings. I believe one of the best things you can do at the loss of a parent, is to evaluate their greatest contribution to your life, magnify it and pass it on through your children.

Gratefully, my father is still living. I tell him constantly that I love him, and how grateful I am to be able to draw upon his knowledge. I dread the day that he will leave this earth. When that happens, I know that I will be terribly sorrowful. I will also know, that I have taken every opportunity to express my love to my dad. That tiny bit of knowledge, I hope, will help me recover.

I saw on TV this morning that fathers are taking on more and more responsibility toward rearing families. I believe this is an excellent statistic.

46

CASKETS 1

EXTERIORS

A casket is a vital component of every funeral service. It expresses dignity, respect and integrity, yet serves a more practical purpose as well. A casket is, "a rigid container which is designed for the encasement of human remains and which is usually constructed of wood, metal, or like material, and ornamented and lined with fabric." (Federal Trade Commission, FTC)

The FTC, as a definition for a casket, publishes the previous statement. There are often misconceptions regarding caskets. In an attempt to clarify these misconceptions, this article will address the outer or main construction materials that make up a casket, and the purposes thereof.

Caskets are simply boxes that hold human remains. While it is true that different caskets have varying options and levels of functionality, they all share the same basic purpose, encasing human remains.

Caskets are constructed of rigid materials. Rigidity is a vital component of a casket. If the bottom and sides of caskets were not rigid, one would be unable to move the decedent from one place to another proficiently and with dignity. The rigidness of the casket allows the funeral personnel and pallbearers to transport the decedent to where it needs to be, in an adequate fashion.

The types of rigid materials used in the construction of caskets vary and each has unique qualities of usefulness. Caskets made of steel, stainless steel, copper or bronze, are very strong. There are various thicknesses of these metals used in casket manufacturing. An important fact to remember is that the smaller the gauge, the thicker the metal. One might ask, "Why does the thickness of metal matter?" I would answer, "In most cases, it does not." The cases in which it will matter depend on the weight of the decedent and the absence of a vault. If a vault is not used and the thickness of the casket is on the thin side, the casket may crush onto the deceased, under the weight of the earth as it is returned and packed into the ground or possibly at a later date as the metal decays.

Another building material used in the manufacturing of caskets is wood. Wood is beautiful, dignified and warm. Caskets made from wood are the most beautiful of all caskets. They can be carved and stained to any request. A wood casket, however, is almost certain to collapse onto the decedent as the earth is returned into the grave. If it does not, wood will be one of the quickest caskets to decay. Once decay begins, the casket will collapse onto the deceased.

A third building material commonly used in casket manufacturing is cardboard. Some companies may call this material pasteboard or corrugated fiberboard or any other combination of those words, but in reality, these caskets are made of cardboard. The same type of cardboard out of which moving boxes are constructed. It goes without saying, without a vault, this type of casket is going to collapse onto the deceased as the earth is returned to the grave.

A newer composition material used in casket manufacturing is fiberglass. This material can be strong and can last for quite some time. In some cases, fiberglass caskets may resemble steel caskets. In choosing this type of casket, one must use one's best judgment and thoroughly inspect the craftsmanship of the fabricator.

In certain areas of the country, green caskets are gaining in popularity. Green caskets are made from a reed type of material, rather like a willow basket. Of course, one knows that baskets crumple easily; therefore, one may deduce that these caskets will readily collapse onto the deceased as the earth is returned to the grave. Green caskets are often more expensive than cardboard caskets, yet function within the same parameters. If you are green minded and want to save funds, the cardboard casket, although not nearly as pleasing to the eye, might be your casket of choice.

Perhaps you have walked through a cemetery and noticed certain graves seem to have fallen or sunken by eight or nine inches. The reason a grave collapses is that having given way under the pressure of the earth's weight, the casket has collapsed onto the deceased. These sunken graves most likely did not utilize the stabilizing features of a grave liner or vault. Some caskets may remain intact for several days, some for several months. Copper or bronze caskets, may stay intact beyond several months. These caskets are rather expensive though, and if one is investing a great amount of money into a casket, one should probably consider protecting that investment with a vault. The fact remains, regardless of the amount of money paid for a casket, without the stabilizing strength of a vault to fortify the grave; your casket will eventually collapse onto the deceased.

Vaults are not required by law; however, some cemeteries may mandate their use. If you have forgone a vault, be aware and mentally prepare for your loved one's grave to collapse in on them, at some point in time. Although optional, a vault is a good investment if you want to preserve the integrity of your loved one's casket.

47

THE EX-FACTOR

As a funeral director, I often experience unique situations with survivors, and this past week was no exception. The family I served was one of humble means. The decedent had experienced interaction with the judicial system on multiple occasions. Drugs had played a part in his life. There was an indication of slowness of mind, and he was potentially murdered. He was a parent with dependent children, and he had an "Ex" wife. Other issues existed as well, but the details are too gruesome to mention, and out of respect to this family, they are better left unwritten.

My motivation for this article is the existence of his "Ex" wife and the discrepancy between her perception of herself, and her legal standing within his estate. My experience and knowledge are based on Texas law and may differ from other states.

Due to the decedent's lifestyle, he did not have an estate, yet his "Ex" wife was very interested in any dependency funds available for her upon his death, and desired to be recognized and respected as his wife.

As I left the cemetery and reflected back upon the week's experience, I thought to myself, how very odd that this woman did not understand her severance from this man, as stipulated through the courts in their divorce decree. Interestingly, this woman is not unique in her misconception of her legal standing within the "Ex" husband's estate. I meet women almost weekly who are under one or more misconceptions regarding their legal status within the estate of a particular male decedent.

It seems as though the popular phrase of the 1960's "It's only a piece of paper," has diluted the legal importance of the marital contract within the minds of many couples. This mere piece of paper is a legal and binding contract, issued through the state which establishes, combines and protects one's legal next of kinship within an estate. If a couple is married, each party is legally recognized as the other's next of kin. As such, each has power, rights and responsibilities within the combined marital estate. Their legal document (marriage certificate) places them in this important position. Individuals who choose to reside together without this legal contract, are not in the next of kinship position, and, therefore, have no legal standing within the estate.

In such a case, a woman who has never been the decedent's legal wife, or who has given up her place as his legal wife, forgoes her rights and considerations as kinship, along with anything else she may consider as combined property and estate. She may therefore find herself evicted from her residence without legal rights to any insurance funds or estate properties. A man however faces far graver consequences. In addition to the previously stated losses, a man who has not married the mother of his children, and has failed to secure his name on their birth certificates, may find that on the dreadful day of losing his pseudo wife, he stands without parental rights. Not only might he lose what he thought was community property, without expensive testing and court battles, he will most likely see the guardianship of his children fall to their maternal grandparents.

The "Ex" wife this weekend wanted the decedent's social security benefits and payouts for her children, as well as for herself. Although her dependent children are possibly eligible for social security funds, she most likely is not. When the marital contract was severed, her privileges and rights were severed too. One hopes she listed her "Ex" husband as the father of her children on their birth certificates; otherwise, they as their mother may be without support.

The key to understanding your position in an estate as spousal next of kin is to understand that there must be a legal and binding contract, a.k.a. a marriage certificate, in effect. If you are an "Ex" spouse, you have been legally removed and displaced as the decedents next of kin. Not only will you have lost all legal claims to the decedent's estate; most probably, you will not be mentioned in the obituary, nor asked to sit with the family at the services. Moreover, if you have forgone the marriage contract altogether, you are not, nor will you ever be, the spousal next of kin.

48

DECORUM

When I was a little girl, I lived in a small town filled with elderly relatives. My relatives would periodically pass away and so at a young age, I had quite a vast knowledge of funeral traditions and funeral etiquette. The first time I became aware that there were "Varying Rules of Etiquette and Tradition" for such an occasion, was at the funeral of my maternal grandfather.

Upon notification that my grandfather had passed away, my paternal grandmother quickly gathered my siblings and me, and off we went to the grand clothing stores in downtown Baton Rouge, LA. I was surprised that I needed special clothing for the event. When I was young, girls were required to wear dresses to school, so I had plenty from which to choose. For some reason, however, although my dresses had always been adequate for funerals in the past, my grandmother felt that they would not do for this particular funeral. She purchased each of us, me and my siblings, beautiful semi-formal clothing. My brother, a beautiful navy suit with a crisp white dress shirt and a dark tie, my sisters and I, each beautiful navy dresses with white patent leather shoes, white anklet socks with lace on them and white patent leather handbags. She also purchased us dainty white gloves and lovely white hats to complete our ensembles. It was rather like Easter, but the clothes were not pastel and the fabrics were heavier and more tailored than usual.

After she was satisfied with our clothes, off we went to Opelousas LA, the location of the funeral home where my mother and her immense family were gathered. Upon arrival, I realized that this funeral was unlike any other funeral I had attended thus far in life. The funeral home was large and filled with my very sad relatives. Of course, sadness is not, in and of itself, unusual at a funeral, but my relatives were overly sad and I attributed their sadness and all of the extra attention toward our clothes and behavior on my grandfather's unusually violent death. I was a child, and although funerals did not bother or confuse me, this funeral was somehow very different, and I just could not quite figure out why. As I grew older, I realized my parents had cultural differences within their marriage, and I was witnessing the variances of culture in its fullest extent, the expression of grief upon the death of a significant loved one.

The funerals I had previously attended were always from my dad's side of the family. His family practiced a gentle Arklatex Christian religion and the funerals were in accordance with their beliefs. This funeral was on my mom's side of the family. Unlike my dad, my mother had been raised a Southern Louisiana Cajun Catholic, and their funerals, as I was about to learn, were very different from the ones to which I was accustomed.

The reason I have shared this with you, is that I am constantly asked by people, "What is appropriate to wear to a funeral?" There is not a simple answer to this question. Clothing and even behavior are predicated on religion, culture and tradition. One should accommodate each funeral to the traditional systems practiced by the grieving family. After all, we go to a funeral to pay our respects. Should we not then practice respect towards the family's religion, culture and traditions? Paying one's respects does not mean that we merely show up and sign the register book. Paying one's respects encompasses a myriad of components. Of course, most of us know that we wear subdued colors, we speak with our quiet voices and one hopes we clean ourselves up before going to the funeral. Many people believe that black is the only color one should wear when in attendance. Although in some groups this is true, in others it is not. For a Buddhist, white is the appropriate color for bereavement.

My basic rule for funeral decorum is the same as it is for attire and language;

> "Be clean, be respectful and be modest."

If you will observe this rule, you should be able to attend almost any funeral and not be offensive to anyone.

49

PET GRIEF

Occasionally, I find letters in my inbox from someone who has read one of my articles. Today was such a day.

Hello Tracy,

We just lost our dog today in an untimely death/accident. I blame myself, and I feel sick, sad, weak, and I've been crying most all of today! It hurts so much when you lose a pet. The pain of loss is so unbearable and never-ending. It will always be with me forever and ever. Do you have any grief briefs concerning pet loss that I could read? I will check your blog, thanks for your help.

Kelly from Alaska

Dear Kelly,

I am so sorry to hear of your pet's death. I have pets myself, and just can't bear to think of the day that they will die. Although I do not know the circumstances of your pet's passing, I wanted to let you know that it is natural to blame yourself when accidents occur. As your pet's custodian, you naturally feel responsible when tragedy occurs. Accidents, however, are called accidents for a very specific reason...they are accidental. Even when accidents are caused through carelessness, they are still accidental. Although one may feel a measure of responsibility in the circumstances; unless one purposefully causes the death of a beloved pet, an accident remains an accident.

I know this does not take the pain away. I have pets that have passed away, and at times, I will think of things I might have done better, that may have prolonged their lives. Unfortunately, there are no do-overs. I have to realize that I have learned to do better, and in my stewardship over my current pets, I will be more alert and proactive.

I am sorry for your loss and know that you will suffer and mull over in your mind the things you wish you had done differently. When this happens, remember the good things you did and the joy you shared with your pet. Eventually, fond memories will override the pain, and you will realize that you are a better person because of the love you shared with your pet, and the lessons you have learned through them.

I do not have pet specific articles because I specialize in human loss. Loss, however, stretches over all life. Grief is the same whether you have lost a pet or person. The depth of grief is based on the depth of love. I know your heart is full of love and very sad right now. I hope you will mend without complications.

Take care and feel free to write me again if you would like.

50

LOVE ME TENDER

"The beauty of Elvis' voice has filled our chapel this morning, the sweetness of his words has filled our hearts, but those of us who have witnessed the love story of Milton and Mona Gay, realize this morning, that even the unparalleled talent of this great vocalist has failed to express its sacred grandeur. "Wow, what an opening statement at a funeral service.

I met my client nearly four years ago as we buried his brother. My client is a kind and dear man in his seventies. Throughout the years, I have seen him around town, and he has never failed to pull a faded and tattered picture from his wallet of his beautiful wife and tell me how much he loves her .Nearly three months ago, my client and his daughter came to my funeral home to make pre-arrangements for his wife.

Late last week, while directing a service for a different family, I received the dreaded call. The nurse on the other end of the line notified me that my client's wife had died. I was heartbroken for him for I knew in his heart, his life had ended as Mona Gay drew, and then released her last breath. Unfortunately, I could not go to the nursing home myself, so I sent my dear husband in my stead to respectfully gather Mona Gay's remains, and bring them back to the funeral home. All through the night, I worried about my client. I knew he was devastated over his loss. Even when one has anticipated the loss of a loved one who has been ill for quite some time, the actual occurrence of death is always dreadful.

Early the following morning, my client came to the funeral home to finalize the details of his beloved's services. As he sat beside me, he reached into his wallet and pulled out the old, faded and tattered picture of his wife, that I had seen on many previous occasions. True as ever, his bright blue eyes radiated deep love as only true love can do. This day was different though, his eyes were bluer, brighter and more deeply radiating as tears ran down his cheeks, and he spoke of his lost love. When it was time to leave, Milton could barely stand. His legs were weak, and his body seemed frail.

Milton and his daughter came early for their visitation. He was hesitant and did not want to see her in her casket. He was so heartbroken and did not think he could bear the anguish of this new life without her. He told me that he thought he might die too, and that his sorrow was too painful to survive. He apologized for crying, not realizing that his tears, his fears and his agonizing sadness were a great honor to his wife.

At the funeral, Milton's strength failed him. He fell to his knees as he approached his beloved's casket for the last moment they would share together. His tears and acclamations of tender love broke my heart, yet renewed my faith that love endures when all else fails.

The beauty of Elvis's voice filled my chapel that morning, and the sweetness of his words filled my heart, but the love I had witnessed from Milton for his beloved Mona Gay will never be expressed through the earthly talent of a great vocalist. Their tender love was one of sacred grandeur.

51

CASKETS II
CARRYING MECHANISMS

The carrying mechanism of a casket is made up of many components. Each component has a unique and specific purpose.

The obvious component of the carrying mechanism is the bar. The bar is the portion of the casket that the pallbearers will grab onto in order to lift and carry the casket from one point to another. Caskets consist of two different bar systems.

The first system is a stationary bar. A stationary bar is fixed and does not move. A stationary bar system is not the most comfortable system for carrying a casket. There is, however, an argument to be made for sturdiness. The stationary bar is very strong and sturdy. In a stationary bar system, the wrists hold most of the weight of the casket and the grip may be painfully stressed. The bar presents a flat shape, failing to provide the pallbearers a substantial gripping surface. I have never seen a stationary bar fail during a service.

The second system is a swing bar. A swing bar moves away from the casket for carrying purposes and tucks back tightly to the casket for esthetics. A swing bar system is more comfortable for the pallbearers. It allows for more room between the casket and the pallbearer's arm and grip. This extra room provides greater leverage, so the pallbearers do not have to lean outwardly from the casket. Standing straight keeps the weight of the casket evenly distributed throughout the pallbearer's body. In so doing, a pallbearer's back is not overly strained, and his wrists are not overly stressed. Of equal importance is the extra room for gripping provided through the outward movement. These precious inches between the casket and swing bar provide skin saving space for the pallbearers hands. The swing bar also has a fuller shape. This fuller shape gives the pallbearer a more substantial gripping surface.

The swing bar is attached to an arm. The arm is the portion that allows for the movement of the bar outwardly from the casket. The arm is quite possibly the most important part of the entire bar system. If the arm is weak, the weight of the casket when carrying a decedent may be cause for alarm. I have only seen one swing bar system too weak to support the weight of the casket during a service. The casket was made by a custom cabinetmaker, and he had purchased the bar system on the internet. The casket carvings and staining were beautiful. All of that paled, however, when the arms failed, and the casket began to awkwardly tilt.

The arm of the casket is attached to the ear of the casket. The ear is not only decorative; it serves to strengthen the area where the entire carrying system attaches to the casket. Without the ear, the ability of the system to carry the weight of the casket and the weight of the decedent would be greatly reduced.

Caskets and casket components have size and weight restrictions. Some of us are fortunate enough to have light loved ones. A light loved one can utilize the least expensive caskets in the funeral home's selection room, internet shopping mall or the casket store's sales floor. If your loved one was a bit portly or extra tall; however, you might consider the advice of your funeral director as invaluable. Unlike a salesperson, a funeral director has had extensive education in funeral traditions, equipment, merchandise and law. His or her knowledge and hands on experience with funeral issues will probably save you tons of anguish and possibly money in the long run. At any rate, advise your funeral director of any issues or concerns you might have about caskets or other funeral merchandise, and he or she will be able to answer or research the answers for you. At least armed with their knowledge and advice, you will be better able to make an informed decision when choosing a casket.

52

FUNERAL DIRECTOR FEARS FOR HER LIFE

Today started out as many do for a funeral director working with broken families, sadly and tragically. Add to this scenario, the loss of a child, and you potentially have a volatile situation on your hands. When I decided to become a funeral director, I did not realize there might come a day I would fear for my life in my own residence, but today was that day. Who knew funeral directing could carry fatal risk? The point is that when life has been lost, emotions are severely heightened; hearts are filled with despair, and anger is uncontrollably prevalent.

It has been my experience, that feuding families strike out at each other and anyone else, who happens to be in their path. Old wounds are ripped asunder with new wounds, and at the time of loss it seems that the downward spiral of despair has the strength of a vortex. Today was not the first time I have been nervous about my safety. It was; however, the first day I feared mortal injury. A grieving giant stood before me, suffering inconsolable agony and mad as a bull over wording in his grandson's obituary. He was truly frightening.

Misunderstandings and tense situations usually surface due to a lack of communication and information between estranged families. Add a death to this mix, and the possibilities are potentially explosive. When families are in the midst of losing a loved one, communicating with each other, or with the funeral home, is not the most important task of the day. Final farewells and precious moments are the critical objective, because, in an instant, they will no longer be possible. In a moment, they will slip away and despair will reside in their stead. Final farewells and precious moments are and should always be; the first and foremost focus of the surviving family, and every funeral director and person outside of the family should understand that.

This man, yesterday, suffered his longest and most dreaded nightmare. No measure of preparation could make that moment anything less that horrific. He had the core of his soul ripped from his aching arms, and there was not a thing he could do to stop it from happening. His heart will never be the same again, nor will his world. He will yearn forever the gentle touch of his grandson's hand, the sweet fragrance of his hair and the precious kiss so gently placed on his angelic cheek. Eventually he will recover to some extent, but life will never be what it was.

Once he is calm and potentially years from now, he will realize that he has been blessed more than others, who have suffered the loss of a child. He does not understand it now, but his blessing was his advanced knowledge that his grandson would pass away from a rare and dreadful disease. Although it is unfair that a child should suffer such a disease and that a family must witness the ravages and loss of their child, he had forewarning that his grandson would prematurely slip from his loving grasp. And that is more than many parents are allotted. His advanced knowledge offered him time to show and express his devotion to his grandson, time to make memories fishing out at the pond and time to make moments count.

I would never want to change places with this grandfather. I am expecting a grandchild myself within the next few months, and I pray incessantly that he will arrive without incident, illness or disease. I cannot imagine the pain and anguish this heartbroken man, who lost his beloved grandson last night, along with all of their future experiences together, is suffering.

My prayers go out to this family. I hope that the pain they suffer will become happy memories of this beloved child, as soon as possible. Their support group is vast, but they have a rough and very sad road ahead of them. Every fiber in their bodies and deep down in their souls ache over this loss, and my soul aches for them.

Tonight friends and family will gather to offer condolences and words of comfort, and preachers will offer words of inspiration. No matter what is said or what is offered, the hearts of this family are so full of sorrow that there is no room for anything else; inspiration and comfort are not possible. There is nothing anyone can say or do, to make this family feel better about what has happened. There is no erasing this tragedy and the pain that comes with it. This family will trudge through despair, and hopefully after great suffering and misery, they will come to a place where they can function and live within this unfair and tragic experience.

I know that everyone coming tonight is searching today for words of comfort to share with this poor family. I am searching myself for some way to help them through this dreadful experience. My best advice would be to allow them to mourn and recover on their own schedule. Offer to be there and support them throughout the coming months which may turn into years, as they work their way from death, back to living. Never become impatient with their sorrow, never abandon them and always provide a path of gentle re-acclamation back to friendship and social acquaintance.

This sorrowful grandpa, so tall in stature and powerful in voice, has been crushed by the fate of death within his family. As we experience the services honoring his beloved grandson over the next few days, I hope that I will be able to protect him from unintended offenses from others and even myself. Nevertheless, if he is overcome with anger and frustration, who wouldn't understand and give him a little latitude. I would rather be intimidated and frightened any day, than walk a mile in his heavy-laden and mournful shoes.

ABOUT THE AUTHOR

Tracy Renee Lee

Tracy Reneé Lee is a funeral director, funeral home owner, Certified Grief Counselor (GC-C), embalmer, syndicated columnist, published author, wife, mother, and grandmother. She enjoys living in East Texas and serving her community with her husband Mike Lee.

www.ingramcontent.com/pod-product-compliance
Lightning Source LLC
Chambersburg PA
CBHW071452070426
42452CB00039B/1138